Ed and Nila Betof

Foreword by Beverly Kaye

Leadership Lessons

FOR ANY OCCASION

Stories of Our Mothers

PRESS

D1214418

ATD Press is an internationally renowned source of insightful and practical
information on talent development, training, and professional development.

ATD Press
1640 King Street
Alexandria, VA 22314 USA

Ordering information: Books published by ATD Press can be purchased by
visiting ATD's website at www.td.org/books or by calling 800.628.2783 or
703.683.8100.

Library of Congress Control Number: 2018950352

ISBN-10: 1-947308-62-9
ISBN-13: 978-1-947308-62-6
e-ISBN: 978-1-947308-63-3

ATD Press Editorial Staff
Director: Kristine Luecker
Manager: Melissa Jones
Community of Practice Manager, Human Capital: Eliza Blanchard
Developmental Editor: Kathryn Stafford
Text Design: Iris Sanchez and Michelle Jose
Cover Design: Spencer Fuller, Faceout Studio

Printed by Versa Press Inc., East Peoria, IL

*To our mothers, from whom we learned
life and leadership lessons that have
enriched our family and our careers.*

*Florence Goodman   1919-1993
Jean Seeger Betof   1922-2002*

Contents

Foreword

When Ed and Nila first approached me about writing this foreword, I initially talked myself out of it. I had many other time-consuming decisions to make and commitments to uphold and I didn't know if I could find the time or energy. Ed and I have known each other professionally for many years. He was a client of my company, Career Systems International, when he led the worldwide talent management and learning functions at Becton Dickinson. We knew of the books each of us had written and of our involvement with organizations such as ASTD (now ATD).

At the time, I was not familiar with Nila's extensive experience as an executive, consultant, coach, and author. Nor had I learned about the wide-ranging influence she has had, especially on senior executive and emerging women leaders, in her role for the past 17 years as chief operating officer of The Leaders Edge/Leaders By Design and as former president of the Forum of Executive Women.

But the very nature of the book really intrigued me, and I have always loved the power of stories for teaching and learning. I also found myself very interested in Nila and Ed—a devoted, dual-career couple who have been married more than 48 years—and the fact that they could write their second book together and survive the experience. Between my own background in career development and engagement, my belief in the power of storytelling, and their dedication to complete this project, I was hooked.

I believe stories are a powerful vehicle to help us reflect on our lives and careers. I use them to drive home important points and to deeply engage others in their work and in their own learning. Stories give us a vivid, memorable way to pass on our values, history, and vision. They help us to understand in ways that are meaningful and relevant. Good stories leave listeners and readers enriched and inspired. They create shared meaning and purpose. They influence, teach, inform, motivate, and uplift. They invoke emotions. They give advice for dealing with adversity and overcoming challenges. They foster understanding. They are, in fact, one of the most effective means of communication. Stories leave a strong impression with listeners and with readers. They tap into our emotions and intellect in ways that help us remember the wisdom of the past as we make informed choices in the future.

Kierkegaard once said that life must be lived forward but can only be understood backward. It's one of my favorite quotes. The stories in *Leadership Lessons for Any Occasion* about mothers and the lasting impact they have had on their adult children not only help us look back on what we've learned from our own mothers, but help us think about the stories we can pass on to our families, our friends, and our co-workers.

Nila and Ed have collected their stories from a wide array of storytellers. The contributors range from young professionals to older adults, and come from many different backgrounds, ethnicities, gender identities, and countries of origin. Most of the stories were written individually; others were co-written by siblings who found it to be a tremendously bonding experience that brought them closer than they had been in years.

No matter their differences, the contributors all seemed to have one thing in common: They looked back on their lives and careers and crystallized important lessons. The stories brought up emotions, thoughts, and feelings that, in some cases, they did not even know they had. More than a few contributors told Ed and Nila that writing their story—in their voice and in their way—was a cathartic experience that was very meaningful to them.

Leadership Lessons for Any Occasion is a book of authentic stories. While it can be read for enjoyment alone, do not be surprised if it causes you to reflect on your own role in life, the effect your mom may have had on you, and the effect you are now having on others. It's also perfect for leaders and those professionals who help teach and develop leaders. Additionally, the reader's guide presents some very specific ideas and methods that you do not want to miss! These ideas can help you use these stories to become a better leader, teacher, and coach.

As you read this book, think about the stories that you have to tell but haven't. Make time for a storytelling experience of your own. I am confident that you will both enjoy and learn from this unique book. It is a tribute to mothers everywhere and to the storyteller in all of us.

—Bev Kaye, Founder, Career Systems International,
now part of Talent Dimensions
December 2018

Introduction

"The most powerful person in the world is the storyteller. The storyteller sets the vision, values, and agenda of an entire generation to come."
—Steve Jobs

Who Wants to Hear a Story?

The year was 2002. I was teaching a career development program to midcareer leaders and professionals. One of the activities required each participant to take a retrospective look at some of the patterns in their careers. But while facilitating this part of the program, I had my own aha moment.

Throughout my career, I've often been asked to start functions, teams, work processes, and programs from scratch, so I've had to be resourceful. I've taken on many fix-it and turnaround challenges, always seeming to end up with tight budgets, limited numbers of people, and inadequate resources. But, I'm not complaining—despite the obstacles, I've always thrived.

That day, while teaching that career development course, I realized—I had learned to be resourceful by watching my mother as I grew up.

My parents had very little money, so we needed to be creative about whatever we had and whatever we did. It was my mother who led the way. About every other night, she would work her alchemy and manufacture four or five quarts of milk out of a single quart. Mom would carefully take the quart of milk that was delivered to our home and divide it into glass and plastic containers. Then she would measure out powdered milk, run water from the faucet, mix it up, and voilà—my three brothers and I had all the milk we could drink.

Saturday was usually hot dog night. There were always more hot dog buns than hot dogs, so on Monday, we could count on finding peanut butter and jelly on a hot dog bun instead of the traditional white bread in our brown bag lunch.

Throw out our worn-out white cotton socks? Never! Our mother had figured out that she could tightly sew several socks together in the form of a ball—and it would never break a window. Let the games begin!

—Ed Betof

Why Stories About Moms?

When we began our exploration into sharing personal stories in our professional teaching and coaching lives, we noted how each story's unique leadership perspective—the essence of what leaders believe, act upon, teach, and expect of themselves and others—could have a positive influence on individuals, teams, and organizations. We have now completed hundreds of interviews with leaders about their lives and career development, and one of the most frequent themes is the influence that mothers and fathers have had on these leaders. Think about it. For many of us, our mothers were the first to sing, read, and tell stories to us. They were our first teachers and coaches. As we grow and mature, we learn to appreciate the power of our mothers' stories, which become part of our developmental history and performance foundation. They stay with us for a lifetime.

Stories work in wondrous ways with people across cultures, ages, and ethnic groups—they connect us. For example, every year we book a hiking trip with a vacation company, and last year's trip was a weeklong stay at the Bay of Fundy in New Brunswick, Canada. There were 16 other hikers from eight different U.S. states in our group. With the exception of two folks we'd met on a previous trip, no one knew one another, including the two guides.

Within minutes of meeting, we began talking about our coming week together, and sharing stories about past hiking trips quickly followed. As the week progressed, we continued sharing stories on the trail, at meals, and at the beautiful inns where we stayed. They were a blend of details—the sites we visited, historical figures, and our own lives and families. One night over dinner, we took the opportunity to share our "mom story" writing project, which eventually culminated in this book. As soon as we finished describing the concept, one of the hikers jumped in with a series of stories about her mother—that was all it took. For much of the rest of the night, our newfound hiking friends shared stories about their mothers, and the sharing continued throughout the rest of the week along the hiking trails and short bus rides. By week's end, we had bonded and learned a lot about one another.

Stories, especially mom stories, have personal and professional impact. In addition to teaching lessons and disseminating information, they also touch the head and heart. We know from experience as well as the more recent findings from the field of neuroscience that an impactful story has a psychological, emotional, and even physical effect. Stories are contagious. If you tell a story that has real meaning or emotionally touches others, you are likely to hear one or more stories in return.

As stories bring people together, they create shared meaning and purpose, and have a bonding effect among people and teams. They help us teach culture, values, and knowledge. They can be used to give advice for dealing with adversity and overcoming challenges. They can be funny, poignant, or sad. They are an important part of fostering ongoing and positive relationships, because they help communicate who you are and what you stand for.

If you have leadership responsibilities, you can use stories to help communicate your unique point of view or perspective on important topics or initiatives. You can use them to inspire others and help lead people into the future.

About This Book

For this book, we sought out the collected wisdom of a wide range of leaders, professionals, teachers, coaches, friends, and talent development professionals about how their mothers guided their paths to helping others lead authentic, resourceful, meaningful lives. *Leadership Lessons for Any Occasion* shares their stories and life lessons. Each of the seven chapters focuses on a different theme that arose as we were reading through the stories. In this book, you'll find stories about developing trust, having a vision, managing change, innovating, being creative; the list goes on.

Leaders and those aspiring to have leadership responsibilities will enjoy and benefit from the stories and lessons of this book. Additionally, the reader's guide at the back will help you better understand how to actively leverage your own people management skills through personalized storytelling. If you are a leader, seek leadership responsibilities, or work in the profession of talent management, leadership, learning, or career development, use these approaches to incorporate mom stories in your work and as you teach and coach others. The essence of our approach is to help you make storytelling easy, and to be able to communicate your leadership perspectives in meaningful ways.

1

First Teaching, Coaching, and Learning

"Experience is the hardest kind of teacher. It gives
you the test first and the lesson afterwards."
—Oscar Wilde

Parenting is the ultimate test of teaching and coaching.

A mother is the first person to bond with her baby, and from the time a child is born, mothers tell them stories. They tell stories about what the world is like, what is important, and how to do things—in other words, they teach and coach. Great leaders do the same. Great leaders inspire others around them by using stories to convey messages and connect emotionally to their audience, whether they are employees, other leaders, board members, or investors.

Mothers never stop teaching. We've been struck by those we have taught and coached, who've told us stories about how their mothers coached and supported their children who grew up to become leaders and professionals. As we prepared to write this book, we remembered a story from Phil Knight's book, *Shoe Dog: A Memoir by the Creator of Nike.* Reflecting on the many ways his mother taught and supported him throughout his career, Knight describes how his mother stood up to his father and lent her son the money he needed to keep his business afloat. Knight's mother played such an important role in his career that he installed a plaque in the entrance of the new athletic facility he donated to the University of Oregon. The plaque reads: Because mothers are our first coaches.

The Rock and the Fish

Sharon Collins Presnell on her mother,
Wanda Collins

I grew up in the foothill region of the North Carolina Blue Ridge Mountains with a wonderful view of Pilot Mountain right in my backyard. We were far from wealthy, but I never realized that until I was much older. We were happy, and we pretty much lived like everyone else. My mother was my teacher until I entered first grade, and in many ways still is today. She taught reading, writing, math, and consequences. The last subject was taught daily, not just in the way I was disciplined, but also through more subtle ways, like when we would sit and tell each other stories. These stories were a gentle way to stimulate my imagination and help recognize and plan for consequences. There was one that we told repeatedly, always a little differently, usually sitting by the neighbor's pond. I would throw a rock in the pond and Mom would ask, "Where did the rock go?"

"To the bottom," I answered.

"What was on the bottom?" she asked. "Use your imagination."

"A fish?"

"Yes! A fish! But . . . poor fish, the rock might have hit him on the head," she would reply. "Next time, let's tell the fish there's a rock coming. What else happened when you threw your rock?"

"There was a big splash."

"See the frogs on the lily pads?" she asked. "They got all wet from the waves. What could we do next time to protect them?"

"Give them all tiny umbrellas," I suggested.

"Yes! That's a great idea."

And on we would go until we had elaborately prepared all the pond creatures for the incoming rocks so they were not surprised or injured when I threw the next one.

Although it's a silly example, it was part of my foundational learning. It showed me the value of recognizing and preparing for consequences—realizing that every word and action, no matter how simple, has the power to have substantial effects on others around us, and that unpleasant consequences can happen when you act without consideration for the impact on others.

As a leader, I began to give out a rock award to people who had disciplined thought and action. Over the years, it has been passed along to individuals who are successful because they planned, were inclusive of others, and thought ahead about the consequences of success and failure—having a clear plan of action for both circumstances.

Building the Basics

Dave Drabot on his mother,
Margaret D. Drabot

We lived on a small farm in northeast Pennsylvania and we were all busy during the day doing our assigned farm chores. Summer evenings, though, offered an opportunity for a little fun. While my father went off to his second job at a local factory, my mother and I would work on my basic baseball skills. She was my first coach and teacher.

When the weather was cooperative, she and I would walk to one of our recently mowed fields with a bat, a glove, and a few battered balls. We would spend an hour or so in the field as she hit a variety of pop flies, line drives, soft ground balls, and hard one-hoppers to me. Before each swing, she'd announce the imaginary game situation, and after I fielded the ball I'd shout out where my throw was intended. She would field my throw with her bare hand, and then quickly launch another ball my way. Sometimes, we'd use the wooden wall of an equipment shed to simulate an outfield fence. She was more than skillful enough to hit a variety of balls to that wall to test my skills.

As we played, my mom would smile if I made a play she thought beyond my capabilities. But if I misplayed a ball or was slow to react, she would not hesitate to point out my lack of hustle. If I got hit by a bad bounce, she would not tolerate any excuses or complaints. It was partly through these evening practices that I learned to accept feedback at an early age.

Afterward, as the sun started to set and the bats filled the sky, she would explain some of the more subtle aspects of the game, such as base stealing, how to properly tag up, how to back up a bag, and how to chatter.

It didn't occur to me that my mother's baseball skills were unique. I thought that all my friends' mothers had a glove and a Willie Mays Louisville Slugger bat. It was only as I grew older and my mother told me the stories of her youth that I understood how she came to love the game.

My mother grew up in a small coal mining town about an hour from our farm. As a little girl, she lived next to a modest baseball field that the local coal company had built. It had stands for a few hundred people and a wooden fence. Like many of that generation, hers was an immigrant family with many children who all wanted to assimilate to American culture. Baseball symbolized America to them, and so they spent their summers on that field. Younger children played in the mornings in unstructured groups. The afternoons were reserved for organized teen summer leagues. The men's leagues, typically composed of coal miners, would play in the evenings. Even if you weren't playing, you were sitting in the stands watching the game and talking to your friends and neighbors.

My mother started learning the basics in grade school, and then continued to play long after. She earned a second-base spot "with the boys" while in high school, taking pride in explaining that she was the only girl in the summer league. During World War II, as most of the men went off to war, she worked at the local sewing factory. She sewed army uniforms by day and played baseball in the evenings with the remaining men in the town. After the war, she married my father and baseball became a memory. However, even years later, my aunts and uncles would all chuckle at family reunions when they recalled my mother's baseball adventures on that coal mining town field.

რ რ რ

I did indeed learn baseball from my mother. But I also learned very early on that anyone can do anything. Mothers can be mothers, but they can also be outstanding baseball players and coaches. My mother made it clear to me that her skills took many hours over many days over many weeks over many summers to evolve. I can still hear her saying "nothing is easy" and "don't get frustrated." I came to see that dedication and proper preparation were two keys to success.

Juggling Big Dreams

Shauna Wilson Betof on her mother,
Diane Wilson

I fell in love with soccer the first time I kicked a ball on my elementary school playground.

In the spring of first grade, I begged my parents to let me join a team. I was like a duck taking to water. Even broken bones couldn't stop me! When I broke my wrist falling off a zipline later that spring, I negotiated with an orthopedist (and my parents' support) to continue playing soccer if I wore a shin pad to protect others from my cast and kept my arm tucked into my stomach. I joined more teams over the next several years, gaining fitness, strength, speed, and skills to match my competitive nature and love of the game. I also managed to break multiple picture frames and crack a door in our family room, but I was never asked to stop playing inside.

I dreamed about playing collegiate soccer, but I had a problem: juggling (keeping the ball in the air by continuously bouncing it on my head, chest, thighs, and feet). I could get a few here and there, but I had a mental block about juggling and it seemed like an unsurmountable obstacle. Some of my teammates were now juggling one hundred times in a row. My mom's suggestion that "it just takes practice" fell on deaf ears. Then one day, she calmly said, "On Saturday, Dad and I are staining the clapboards on the house. You will juggle to 100."

Over the next couple days, I experienced fear, nervousness, and self-doubt. I created lots of excuses, but my mom was there with positive words and an unshakable belief in me. When Saturday arrived, to put it mildly, I was a wreck.

As she set up the ladder, brushes, and stain with my dad, she called out, "Grab your ball Shauna—try and get to 10."

Piece of cake . . . first hurdle navigated.

"OK, now 20."

On and on I went until 70 times in a row was a routine thing.

Now, my belief joined hers. A persistence and commitment to go for my dream—both learned from my mom—took over. Periodically I called out the new high number and got a word of encouragement in response. That afternoon, I broke 120.

Today, goal setting and persistence have helped me achieve some of my biggest dreams.

Small House, Big Home Warmth

Michael J. Mersky on his mother, Rose Mersky

My mother, Rose, was a typical Jewish mother and wife, whose world revolved around her children and her husband. My dad, Charlie, never wavered in his support for my mother; she was first in his life, well ahead of his three children. Before I became a father, he told me, "The greatest gift you can give to your children is to love their mother."

On any given Friday or Saturday night, when I longed to go to my friends' homes and hang out, they would always reply, "Mersk, let's go to your house."

I never quite understood why they wanted to come to my house until I realized that they wanted to spend time with my mom in the kitchen. In our home, the kitchen was the hub, even though there was barely enough room to walk around. It was only as big as a modern walk-in closet, with a kitchen table and enough chairs to seat five or six people. What made it special was whatever Rose Mersky was cooking at the time—chicken soup, pea soup, hot roast beef sandwiches, and her special stuffing in cupcake tins in the winter; chopped chicken liver, chilled fresh fruit, homemade cakes, and special milkshakes in the summer.

We would crowd into her kitchen, and she loved every minute of it. She listened to the banter and never let on that she heard anything.

What my mom created, I am sure, was planned. She created love and warmth for all who visited. My buddies would spend endless hours in that kitchen. My mom made them feel special, enveloping them with love, a caring and warm atmosphere, and, yes, great homemade food. And for your average 16-year-old boys, there was nothing better than Momma Mersky's kitchen.

The great lessons I have carried with me throughout my career in educational leadership have two main ingredients—courage and love. I learned both in that little rowhouse from my parents.

Ice Skating With Mom: My First Leadership Lesson

Wendy York Witterschein on her mother,
Margaret Halpin York

I remember ice skating with my Brownie troop at Rogers Stadium in Harrison, New Jersey. It was very cold. Our mothers were huddled together on the bleachers in their wool hats and scarves, their mittens wrapped around cups of hot coffee. Their frosted breath was visible as they chatted and laughed.

But my own mother was nowhere to be found on those bleachers. Instead she was ice skating with my friends and me. She was having fun, talking and laughing with us, getting to know my friends, sharing their hopes and dreams, and building trust.

Although at age 10 I was not thinking of leadership, I later realized that this was my first true leadership lesson. Only through strong personal relationships can leaders build trust with their team members.

Mother Knows Best

Alejandra Love on her mother, Cheryl Mayers

My mother comes from Barbados in the West Indies. If you are not familiar with West Indian parenting it can be summarized as follows: Big on respect and low on explanations because Mother *always* knows best.

One of the many things my mother knew was that I would be the first in my family to attend and graduate from college. She was a 4.0 student, but had me straight out of high school, so her own postsecondary degree came from the prestigious University of Motherhood. However, she wanted something different for me, something that would open a world of opportunities. My mother told me I was going to college long before I could spell college or understand what it was.

When the time finally came for me to start looking at colleges, I went to the counselor's office and grabbed every booklet, application, and open house flyer I could find. I had pretty good grades but a very bad attitude, one that had often gotten me in trouble with the administration, teachers, and other students. I ran home from school, plopped on my bedroom floor, read every piece of paper, looked at the mess I'd created, burst into tears, and essentially decided to live at home and work in fast food forever.

At this point my mom's senses must have started to tingle because she walked in just as I gave up. I explained that it was too much. I was completely overwhelmed by the process. After talking me out of a career in fast food, she hugged me tight, looked me in the eyes, and said, "I have no idea how to do this college stuff, but we don't have to do it alone."

At this point I was in a state of shock. I'd never heard my mother say "I don't know" in my entire 17 years of life. And while I knew (logically) that she couldn't know everything, up to this point she had never been wrong or unsure about anything.

The next morning we walked into the school counselor's office and asked every question we could think of. That day I learned it's OK to ask for help because the smartest people don't do it alone. My mother showed me how to use the resources available to accomplish my goals. With her support, I attended college and now hold a bachelor of arts and master of public administration; with her continued support, I'm now working on advanced certifications.

My mom's determination to help me achieve my college dream completely changed the trajectory of my life. I've been able to help hundreds of children apply to college through my volunteer work. And, as an adult educator, I influence the lives of thousands of children every year. My mom knew I would go to college; she pushed me through every doubt, guided me through every step, and supported me until the goal was accomplished.

I guess Mother really does know best.

2

Developing and Supporting Others

"If you're not making someone else's life better,
then you're wasting your time. Your life will
become better by making other lives better."
—Will Smith

Mothers begin providing support to their children long before a baby is born. As her child grows, she identifies where her child needs help and where they need to develop independence. Mothers support their children as they learn life's dos, don'ts, and values during childhood and teenage years. These lessons frequently form the foundation of the leadership beliefs and skills we need throughout our lives.

Often, when leaders look back on their lives and careers, they realize how invaluable their mother's support has been and the many forms it has come in. Sometimes Mom provided a thoughtful suggestion at just the right time. Or maybe it was lending a helping hand, providing resources, or demonstrating trust and confidence when it was most needed. Often without knowing it, mothers have successfully practiced situational leadership. Effective leaders know, as do mothers, that providing support when it's needed can go a long way in helping someone develop and perform at high levels. Leaders identify where they should step in to support the development of their team members and where they need to step back and support from behind.

Mothers don't only provide support in the home. We see them supporting others at work and on school boards, acting as community and business development leaders, and serving in elected offices. Their support of others is the basis of their impact and positive influence in these settings.

Gathering at the Edge of the Table

David Smith on his mother, Connie Smith

I learned some important lessons from my parents growing up. We moved about every five years, and that alone teaches you about loneliness and independence. However, it was as I entered high school that I learned some important lessons from my mother about caring for people, love, empathy, and what can happen when you look for those who gather at the edge of the table. Oh, we all know them; they usually sneak in with the rest of the crowd, try to remain quiet, and stay out of the way of others.

My two brothers and I were busy with school and other activities, so, looking for something to fill her time, my mother began to substitute teach. Like many high schools across the country, mine was made up of all kinds of kids with all kinds of economic backgrounds. Some kids had enough money to eat every day, some brought their lunch, and some just waited until it was time to go home.

Now, my mother taught me many things, and one of those was about being hospitable. Even now, if someone comes to my house to visit, do work, or try to sell me something, I'll likely offer them water or sweet tea to drink. If she noticed a student avoiding the cafeteria or sitting without anything to eat, she would do her best to give them money or buy them lunch, whichever was the least noticeable. She always spoke to them like they mattered, knew their names, approached the scenario with dignity, and never called it a loan. And, these occurrences weren't random; she didn't simply stumble upon those students, she was looking for them.

As I watched her work with funny kids, bad kids, good kids, and, well, just kids, I learned how important it was to always look toward the edge of the table—to look to those who don't fit in or aren't involved, and seek them out. I used this lesson when I was in school, swapping the title of "new kid" with others. I befriended them until they made their own friends, and always made sure to offer them a seat, some simple conversation, or help.

Now that I work in human resources, I use that lesson in my work every day. I am passionate about problem solving, but know that my desire to help must be met with genuine care that is easily translatable. After all, most folks don't just let you in. It takes some time and you have to prove yourself.

Meticulous Ways

Angel Livas on her mother, Veronica Todd

If you know anything about having to vacuum the living room (that nobody goes into)—just for the sake of the room having fresh lines—then you might understand just how meticulous the Todd household was kept.

As the middle child of three, and the oldest daughter, I always felt like it was my job to be second in command for the execution of our family gatherings. Mom seemed to be a little obsessive-compulsive because everything needed to be perfect. All the silver had to be brilliantly polished (and a speckle of tarnish was unacceptable). The entire house had to be freshly vacuumed (even the rooms where no one was permitted). And there were rules for where we could play with our cousins.

But she had a purpose. At the end of the day, it was all about creating a beautiful experience for our guests.

As a child, I couldn't understand my mother's desire to engineer every situation with such precision. But it became clearer as I grew up, especially when I planned my first event for women entrepreneurs. Nearly 150 women business owners registered, and I could not have been more excited. While it was my first large event, I found that it didn't feel any different from planning a large dinner for my family. Thankfully, I didn't have to vacuum or polish silverware. But the lessons I learned from those tasks—precise planning and meticulous attention to detail—prepared me to execute well-strategized events.

My mom poured everything she had into those dinners, and I'm proud to have gained that same level of precision in caring about the experience I create for every event that I execute.

Always in Action

Dodi Fordham on her mother,
Doris Myers Fordham

My mother inspired others by action—and she was always "in action."

In 1972, a nearby town was devastated by Hurricane Agnes. Despite historic flooding and calls for evacuations, many families chose to stay. I remember some friends staying at our house for a few nights to have a dry place to sleep. Others came to do laundry because the water had flooded their homes.

At the time, there was no federal or state assistance—in fact, this was the storm that led to the creation of the Federal Emergency Management Agency (FEMA). We relied on our neighbors for help. There were power outages everywhere, and with the loss of pumping stations, no drinking water either.

My parents were horse farmers, but we were surrounded by dairy farms. So, Mom had the idea to get all the local dairy farmers to loan their sanitary bulk milk cans to bring water to those in need. She encouraged everyone who had been spared the rising flood waters to pitch in. They filled the giant containers with drinking water—the most immediate need—and anyone who had trucks to transport those heavy cans either loaned them to others or drove them into Wilkes-Barre.

That action was necessitated by a disaster that needed immediate attention, but my mother was always helping others through her involvement in local organizations, such as the United Way, the Junior League, and other civic groups. Later in life, she found a new passion: art and helping artists launch their careers. When my mom discovered the need for emerging artists to not only have a place to show their work, but have a mentor to guide them through the fundamentals of an art career, she opened an art gallery to provide a venue for them. That was a 15-year endeavor that many artists credit with giving them the confidence to pursue their own passion.

I have tried to follow in my mother's footsteps through civic activities in a number of charities, especially for artists. Through my mother, I learned the importance of helping others.

Making Each Moment Matter

Teresa Roche on her mother, Virginia M. Roche

My mom was a leader everywhere she was. During World War II, she gave birth to my eldest brother shortly before my dad was declared a POW, but that didn't stop her from keeping her family fed. Later, after Dad returned home, she talked the gas company into keeping our service going after discovering the bill hadn't been paid in several months. And then, after my parents got divorced, my mom bought her own house.

When I started kindergarten, Mom decided to go back to work for the first time in 18 years. She had also stopped driving for 15 years, which I think my siblings and I had something to do with because being in a car with seven children could be a bit much for anyone. However, my mom got her driver's license again and bought a car.

Despite what life brought her, my mom always responded with equanimity and grace. I often observed her asking powerful questions and listening deeply without judgment. She was direct and loving in her feedback to others. These were important leadership lessons for me. Watching her shaped my ability to help others to learn, grow, and succeed. My mom was the first developer of talent I knew. She taught me how to live fully, remain curious, love deeply, and make each moment matter. I could not have asked for a better first coach.

When Food Is More Than Food

Jean Larkin on her mother, Jean Sussmann

My mom was a master cook who transformed her passion for food into her own catering business. Friends first recognized my mom's talent when they ate at our house. She didn't have special training, but she learned by doing and developed special relationships with her customers. Over the years, brides and grooms, satisfied guests, and others who hired her for special occasions would pass through our kitchen to praise my mom and her meals.

Her business included us, too. My sister, brothers, and I all worked alongside her. My dad would join in on the weekends or whenever he could. I remember us all sitting around the table rolling hundreds of bite-size meatballs. My brothers were so small when they first started out that they had to stand on plastic egg crates to reach the sinks to help with dishes.

The skills I learned as a teenager in food prep and as a waitress enabled me to support myself and pay for my college education. My mother's catering business was hard work, but it was also a way for her to express love and connectedness. She started her business out of financial need, and it provided important income, but she also wanted our family to be together and loved watching others enjoy what she prepared.

I appreciated how my mother used what she was passionate about to offer and share it with others to make their lives better. As I watched her create and develop her business, using her own imagination, skills, hard work, and determination, I began developing my own work skills, always confident that I could be successful at what I chose to do, too.

My Mother, the HR Department

Peter J. Dean on his mother, Helen Dean

On December 8, 1941, the day after the Japanese attack on Pearl Harbor, my grandfather and father enlisted in the U.S. Marine Corps. My grandfather was assigned duty training troops in Rhode Island, and my father was assigned a tour in the Pacific as a combat marine, landing on three islands controlled by the Japanese. At home, my grandmother got a job as a spot welder.

The war ended in 1945, and I was born on December 7, 1946. My father told tales of heroic leadership around the dinner table, and the stories often signified the leadership qualities of focused energy, taking initiative, decisiveness, and the drive to get things done. His experience in World War II clearly showed him certain qualities that were aligned with my understanding of leadership.

But my understanding of leadership would not be complete where it not for my mother.

She was a recognized and successful dress designer who chose to stay at home to manage my four siblings and me. Time and time again, she would engage people by giving them her full attention, listening without judgment, questioning and paraphrasing when she did not understand something fully, practicing empathy by truly seeing what the other person was saying, and showing intrinsic respect for the other person. Then she would speak with humor, insight, and a willingness to help. I later realized that she was essentially the HR director of our entire extended family.

Learning to "Work the Room"

Craig Weakley on his mother, Nancy Weakley

My mother has a very distinct way of introducing herself at gatherings. There is almost a regal tone to the way she says, "Hello, I'm Nancy Weakley." But her introduction is only the beginning. My mother knows how to work the room.

As far back as elementary school, I remember my mother gliding from family to family in the stands of my basketball games or at school fundraisers. She grew up in a modest middle class home in Decatur, Illinois, but there was nothing "small town" about her. My mother's demeanor was not about being superior to others; it was simply about being welcoming, fitting in. She would smile and look you in the eye, always putting a new acquaintance at ease. It wasn't phony. There was always a sincere desire for her to get to know her new friend just a little better.

And she taught me how to work the room, too! This has proven extremely valuable, and I can't imagine my own life or career without learning this essential lesson from her.

Running on Empathy

James P. Orlando on his mother,
Cynthia A. Orlando

I was out for an early morning run when I saw an iPhone, wallet, and keys scattered in the middle of the street. It was as if they were accidentally placed on top of a car and someone drove off forgetting they were there. I picked them up. Nothing was broken. The phone had a full charge. It looked like it had just happened. At first, I placed them on the curb, figuring that someone would surely return quickly to retrieve them (on average, people look at their cell phone every six to seven minutes). However, after a few minutes of push-ups, I realized that no one had shown up.

I was annoyed. It had been days since my last run, and work was particularly stressful. I was torn between wanting to run for my health and wanting to help. Then, I began to think, "What if these were my valuables? How would I feel if I lost them? What would I want a stranger to do if they had found my cell phone, wallet, and keys lying in the middle of the street?" Of course, I would be cognitively hijacked for hours and likely dwell on my carelessness over the following days. So, I decided not to leave these items on the curb any longer. I peeked into the wallet and found the address on the driver's license, which was not too far away. Cutting my run short, I went back to my house, dropped the items in a plastic bag, and got ready for work. When I reached the address on the license, no one was home, so I left the items along with my business card on the front porch.

As I drove to work, I wondered why I left my business card. I knew that I wanted to know that the owner actually got the items. This would close the loop for the day and give us both relief. But there was also the potential jolt of positive energy and happiness that comes from doing a good deed for others. When the thankful owner called me later, I could hear the joy and relief in his voice. What a small, but not insignificant, emotional lift for me, too, knowing that I made his day.

My mother taught me to "think about how other people would feel" and to "put yourself in their shoes." When I was growing up, friends would come over to talk with her, and I remember her sitting at the kitchen table with her cup of coffee, nodding and interjecting a few words here and there, but listening more than talking. Victor Frankel wrote in his book *Man's Search for Meaning* that suffering is like gas in a chamber. No matter how large or small the chamber, the gas will fill it. Thomas Jefferson is credited with saying, "When you listen to others, you divide up the suffering in the world and make it a bit easier for them and the world to manage." That was what my mom was doing when she would take time to listen to others. She was a busy person. She made and sold bagel baskets out of our basement (Christmas was especially busy), she was a beautician, and she was studying to get her business associate's degree. I learned from my mom that no matter how busy we are, we can also take time out to be empathetic to others.

Praise and Consequences

Jim Ozello on his mother, Carol Schiller

When my mom got divorced in 1937, she had a nine-month-old son. At the time, scarcely anyone was divorced, and certainly no one that she knew or had even heard about. But she went to work every day, raised me (her only child), and didn't complain. I learned at an early age to be very responsible. I would start dinner for us, so that when my mother got home from work we could eat together. This was one of my favorite times with my mother.

I remember my mom telling me how pleased she was when she found me doing something right or nice. And that praise inspired me to do "the right thing" or "the nice thing" when there was an opportunity to do so. Doing something good or nice for others made me feel good, and made me feel good about myself. That concept was so ingrained in me by her, that the "good" behavior simply became a matter of fact—not because you would be praised for it, but because "it was just the right thing to do." This has been a leadership lesson in building my business relationships throughout my career.

There Is Joy in Work

Donna Boles on her mother, Frances Boles

My mother and father both were hard, dedicated workers who actually met on the job. They worked at the local supermarket right across the street from our house. My brother and I could walk to the store and see our mom in action every day. She got a lot of respect from her fellow workers as well as her bosses. She always showed up for work on time, only missed time due to serious illness, and always wore a smile. Wearing a smile in a retail business that many people come through every day, every hour is no small feat. However, Mom loved her job so much that she said it was not like being at work. She even developed personal relationships with her regular customers. They would come into this big supermarket looking for Frances and would yell "hello" to her from the door.

From watching my mom, I knew I had to go into an occupation that would bring me joy. I wanted to get up every day with a smile on my face to go earn my living. It had such an impact on my brother and me that we both requested to work at our mom's supermarket on our 16th birthdays. The supermarket complied, and I literally started working at the store on my 16th birthday! I, like my mom, took so much pride in my work, and the many relationships I developed from that experience.

Magnetizing Compassion

Cheryl Wood on her mother, Joyce Swann

My mother often put herself in other people's shoes. Despite being a woman of little means, she worked hard to support others who were in need of help. She was a single parent raising three young children in an inner-city housing project on the minimum-wage salary of a public school system employee. But that did not stop her. She never simply wished someone well—she went out of her way to demonstrate kindness; a hot meal to a complete stranger, an envelope with a few dollars for someone else, a ride to a friend who needed it, or just being there for a person experiencing a life challenge.

My mother would say, "Always practice the golden rule because what goes around comes around." There were countless occasions I remember my mom taking us to the store to purchase groceries for other families who were in need. And I would think to myself, how can we help anybody else when we are barely surviving? I now believe we always had everything we needed because of my mother's compassion for others. She magnetized compassion to herself because of the compassion she demonstrated for others.

Barbara Had Flair

Alicia E. Daugherty on her mother,
Barbara C. Hushion

My mother, Barbara, was glamorous, funny, and in many ways bigger than life. She loved to entertain—whether it was throwing lavish parties at our home, or on the stage in our annual parish musical productions. She didn't just play Mame, she was Mame!

To both my delight and chagrin, my mother taught at my high school. Barbara was well loved so I had it easier than the children of less popular teachers. But she was always *there*. Laughing, talking, and sometimes singing. The other kids thought it was adorable—I found it mortifying.

Barbara was very fancy. She wore suits and dresses to school every day. She favored bright colors and elaborate costume jewelry. She was the only woman I knew who could carry off feathers. She never left the house without lipstick, was always put together, and, in the company of anyone but immediate family, always wore a smile. She never owned a pair of jeans.

When I was a teenager, I found her personal flair to be a constant source of embarrassment. I couldn't understand why she had to draw attention to herself—why she couldn't just be normal like my friends' moms. I called it vanity, and generally limited my own style to whatever everyone else was wearing. Her advice that "it's better to be over-dressed than under-dressed" fell on deaf ears.

If we would see a woman with curlers in her hair, my mother would say "Where is she going later that's more important than where she is now?" I would reply, "She's probably going to a fancy party and now she's just at the grocery store." But my mother insisted that whoever was at that party was no more important than the clerk at the store. I eventually came to realize that the care she took in her appearance, and her tendency to laugh and joke and break into song, was less about making herself special, and more about showing other people that they were special.

Because of my mother I strive to always present my best self, regardless of the audience. I take care in my appearance as a way to show others that I care. I laugh and joke and occasionally break into song. Though I rarely wear feathers, I always wear lipstick, and, of course, I never wear curlers.

Ultimate Village Screener

Gilbert "Chuck" Davis on his mother,
Thelma Davis-Spurill

Until I was about 10 years old I lived in a row house full of people, and I was the only child. It wasn't just my immediate and extended family; there was also a host of multiple boarders. With all the "riffraff" around, there were shenanigans happening on a daily basis. But my mom made sure I was protected from it all. She would only leave me in the supervision of an adult whom she trusted, and her screening was off the charts: "Do you get high?" "Do you smoke reefer?" "Do you smoke cigarettes?" "Who are you sleeping with?" "Where do you work?" "Where do you go to school?" "Who will be in the house with you?" "Do you drink?" And the list went on! And these were just questions for our family. Others got it worse. If they didn't pass with flying colors, my mom would simply take me with her or not go at all if she could help it. You know the saying "it takes a village to raise a child"? Well, my mom should have been nicknamed the ultimate village screener! She was extremely selective of whom she allowed in my presence and their role in my life.

My mother's mentality taught me how important it is to take personal accountability for being a good steward of resources and assets. As a result, I am ultra-protective and selective about whom I let represent my company and its brand. The ultimate screener concept has allowed me to be more diligent in the critical thinking and decision-making processes required to build a high-achieving team. It has given me an innate ability to "feel people out" quickly and assess their interests without overanalyzing the situation. Whenever I've used this approach, I've always known I made the right decision.

3

Having Vision
and Hope

"A vision is not just a picture of what could be;
it is an appeal to our better selves, a call
to become something more."
—Rosabeth Moss Kanter

Children and families face what sometimes can feel like an endless array of challenges. Health issues, financial instability, peer pressure, learning barriers, alcohol and drugs, and a lack of consistent parenting are just a few examples of challenges that young people and families have to overcome. Mothers often become the stabilizing force in their families. Whether a child or family crisis, just trying to survive, or aspiring to be all they can be, it is often moms who provide a compelling vision and hope for the future. They help their families see beyond their short-term circumstances and commitments to imagine and achieve a more meaningful future.

Business and organizational leaders must also engage their people around common goals and a desired, envisioned future. Similar to mothers with their families, organizational leaders have to create an environment where excitement and hope fuel the achievement of goals that might otherwise seem unattainable. Like mothers, leaders must create big, inspiring ideas supported by deeply understood and embraced values and goals. They must also be able to communicate their message and story in ways that all understand to embrace a common path forward. Vision can create hope and hope can generate inspired action.

The stories in this chapter are written by professionals and leaders who have experienced successful careers and whose mothers helped create a vision for their lives and a sense of hope for their futures. Their mothers did whatever it took. Some employed faith and others rigor and discipline. They all inspired their daughters and sons to be all they could be.

Whatever It Takes

Renee Owens Kennish on her
mother, Veda Owens

My mom was a complex woman. I always wondered how her younger years affected her adulthood. Her father was blinded when she was an infant, and her mother died when she was five years old. She was raised by her grandparents and an aunt and uncle. She grew up to be a very pessimistic woman—she had a bit of an inferiority complex and was stubborn, at least with our family. However, when she was in a social situation where she felt comfortable, she was much different. She laughed and was fun, not negative at all. Most of my close friends thought she was a lovely woman, sweet, kind, deferential.

I wanted to be the opposite of my mom. I wanted to be positive, confident, and optimistic. I refused to be cynical and gloomy. And I believe I was relatively successful. But, her stubbornness! I couldn't shake that trait. Or perhaps, perseverance or determination would be putting a more positive spin on that characteristic.

When I was five, I was diagnosed with a chronic and severe kidney disease that my parents were told was terminal. Doctors said I wouldn't live past my 20s, but my mother would hear nothing of that. She was committed to my health and ultimate longevity. She was tenacious—taking me to doctor after doctor in her efforts to find one who would work with her to improve my odds of beating the disease. Some gave her no hope. But she persevered and found a doctor who gave her a diet for me to follow, rules around keeping me free of other illnesses that would have a negative impact on my kidneys, and generally hope for my future. My mom was diligent, always cooking two meals—one for the family and one for me. She made sure I followed all the doctor's orders. She never slipped in her determination, not once. And all of this was before grocery stores were laden with special dietary products. But it worked. Her determination saved my life, literally! I turned 70 this fall.

In the end, a trait I may have seen as negative turned out to be very positive. Throughout my career, I've taken on many difficult assignments and have worked to see the positives rather than the negatives in each. I can only hope that I have the courage and fortitude to be as tenacious as she was when faced with a life-altering challenge.

The Power of Faith

Douglas N. Clayton on his
mother, Anne Saad Clayton

Anne rarely accompanied her seven children to Sunday mass. That was our father's responsibility. Staying home while we were at church gave her a couple hours of well-deserved quiet time. However, we knew our mother was a woman of faith. She taught us how to say our prayers by repeating them with us every night while we lay in bed. She made sure that we attended catechism class on Wednesday afternoons.

Her most notable act of faith, however, occurred during the summer of 1976, as my 13-year-old sister, Dianne, lay in a coma after falling off her bicycle. It was her fifth day in the hospital, and only the efforts of doctors, nurses, and technicians kept her breathing. My mother cared for her around the clock, while my brother and sisters kept her strong with emotional support. Our aunts, uncles, and friends prayed for her. We were all stunned when my parents told us that our youngest sibling would have to undergo high-risk brain surgery the next morning. It was a life-or-death situation.

That night, my mother placed a scapular underneath my sister's pillow and breathed the prayers that only mothers can—prayers from the depths of her soul. As the doctors entered Dianne's room to begin preparations for surgery, she woke out of the coma. The doctors were practically speechless—they eventually declared Dianne's awakening as a miracle because they could find no medical explanation. The faith and prayers whispered by our mother proved to be a valuable lesson in belief and hope that we'll all keep with us for the rest of our lives.

I Will Not Just Survive, I Will Thrive

---

*Maqsood Mamawala on his
mother, Munira Mamawala*

At age 72, my mother left behind her brothers, sisters, friends, and religious community in India to move to the United States with my dad. Before she left, she gave away all her belongings, including clothes, furniture, and keepsakes from a lifetime in her native land.

She identified the specific people she had in mind to give particular items. For example, she decided that the fancy tea set (used only for special company) would go to a sister-in-law who had always admired it. She gifted her favorite purses to a family friend who had envied them. A set of mugs and coffee cups were carefully distributed among her many cousins and my father's friends. She fit what was left—a life's worth of possessions—into two bags.

Meanwhile, we were preparing a home for them state-side. And while I'd like to think we anticipated their needs and bought them everything we thought they needed, I continue to be amazed at how they handled the change. New country, new culture, new stuff. Even at home, Mummy had to figure out how to use new appliances like the washer and dryer, vacuum cleaner, and coffee maker, which we all take for granted. She overcame these challenges without complaint, and always with a kind word and smile. Her trademark sense of humor survived the trip.

My mother's positive attitude toward life proclaimed "come what may, I will not just survive, I will thrive!" It has provided so many clear guideposts and for that I am eternally grateful and thankful.

Support, Insight, and Faith

Robert Betof on his mother, Jean Seeger Betof

As a young boy growing up in the city, I found numerous ways of getting into trouble and causing concern for my parents. In school, my teachers moved me to the front of the classroom to keep better watch over my impulsive behaviors. My mother knew that I needed some guidance before I really went off the rails, but she also thought I needed something more than discipline. When I was nine, she concluded that what I needed was a creative outlet. I liked to draw and paint, and my grade school teachers reported that art class was the only time I was focused and under control in the classroom.

So, Mom decided to sign me up for Saturday morning art classes. Because the classes were a long way from home, and we didn't have a family car, we took the trolley to get there. After taking me to class for a couple weeks, my mother determined that I knew how to get there on my own, so she purchased some trolley tokens and trusted me to go to class and return home safely. She also gave me some very strict guidelines and made sure I observed them.

These classes ignited a passion within me, but it's thanks to my mother that I discovered it. The outcome was that I not only greatly benefited from the classes, but was trusted to do it on my own and be accountable. Years later, I received a four-year scholarship to the Pennsylvania Academy of the Fine Arts.

I have now had a long career as an artist. I've also been a program leader at The Y and camps as a swimming coach, and I worked for many years with children who have physical, intellectual, and emotional limitations. My professional and leadership success is grounded in the trust that others placed in me. That trust, to a large extent, was established through the support I provided to colleagues, team members, and those we served. It was a lesson first learned at the age of nine, when my mother let me ride the trolley across town to attend Saturday morning art class.

How a Lifeguard Became a Cheerleader

John Gillis Jr. on his mother,
Carolyn Moxley Gillis

In 10th grade I switched from being an offensive lineman on the high school football team to being a member of the cheerleading squad. I then went on to cheer at the University of Texas during my undergrad, to coach at Baylor University as a graduate assistant to pay for my MBA, to perform at the opening ceremonies of the 1996 Olympics in Atlanta, to travel from Japan to Mexico, and to meet my wife through the sport. Cheerleading became a very unexpected, very large part of my life. Yet, my biggest cheerleader was my mom.

Whenever I fell—whether it was not winning the elementary school talent show or losing the student council election in junior high or just general disappointment from rejection—my mother helped me get back up. Through conversation and questions, we processed my feelings and expectations on each situation. I learned from each one and moved on.

Now with my own children, I realize how many times they try, and how each time puts them in a position of joy—or defeat. For example, after training for many years, my oldest son did not make the school soccer team. My second child is an aspiring actor, going to many auditions yet rarely receiving the role. My daughters are gymnasts and have only received one perfect 10 in competition; every other time they are critiqued.

Just like I did, they fall. Yet, they're never down for long. I credit my mother for that. She helped me manage my disappointment and sorrow, and I like to think I've passed that on to my children. I did not wallow; instead, I received a mental life raft. My mom was my lifeguard.

My Asian Tiger Mom

Sabrina Kay on her mother, Kum Sun Kim

I grew up in South Korea with a stereotypical Asian mother. My dad was a romantic, but Mother was the highest level of Tiger Mom that all the books talk about. Growing up, I didn't understand why my mother was so tough on me.

Korea has monthly exams to help prepare students for university entrance exams. If I got an A- in any class, my mother would come and sleep in my bed for the whole month, taking up the entire bed, so that I would not be able to sleep and be forced to study all night. She would get up in the middle of the night to make sure I was still studying. She brought me milk and cookies to encourage me. As soon as she fell asleep, often around 2 a.m., I would doodle, because my brain was too fried to do anything else. I became quite a good illustrator from that nightly doodling. It's how I became a fashion designer.

My mother also had "might as well" disease. She'd always say, "While you're at it, you might as well do more." I took that message to heart. When I retired in my 30s and became a philanthropist, I figured that I "might as well" serve on more than 30 charitable boards. I never stopped working hard to give back to this amazing country that provided so much opportunity to me and my family. The focus, discipline, and tenacity my mother instilled in me made me who I am today.

A Relentless Love

Chris Cappy on his mother, Virginia Cappy

A few months before she passed away, I gave my mother a little spiral-bound black book. I asked her to write things that had helped her live her life, and things that might help me, too. The project was also to help her regain that perfect Palmer penmanship after yet another small stroke. After every setback, even at this stage of the game, my mother refocused on using whatever she had left.

> *There are no guarantees in life. See opportunity in every failure. The road to success is always under construction.*

My mother and I became best friends due to our circumstances. My childhood years were dominated by a car crash that put her husband, my dad, into a monthlong coma. When he came out, he was a different person—going from being an outgoing friend to the world to an increasingly erratic guy who drank and smoked too much. I was four when it happened. The 10 years that followed were completely unpredictable. Every two or three weeks he would disappear to drink, sometimes all night, sometimes coming home earlier in a cocktail of moods and mixed feelings that scared everybody. This pattern careened through troubles with the law, the church, his friends, our neighbors, and in our home. Each episode was always followed by my father's profound remorse and an increasing tendency to not remember what had happened.

My grandparents owned a liquor store that my mom had grown up working in. She'd seen a load of grief growing up in the Depression, and she made a choice early on not to drink. Instead, she turned to God. Through everything that happened with my dad, she continued to tell my sister and me to love him—no matter what. She wanted us to realize he had become sick and to appreciate what we had. She somehow stayed optimistic through it all, saying often that our love would somehow get us through. She kept finding ways to keep things together—at points barely after going back to work full-time—and to manage her own fears and loneliness by remaining gracious and grateful no matter what. There was never any blame or resentment or anger.

> Love is God. Love is a feeling of harmony.
> Love is accepting as is. Love is kindness and
> caring toward others. First love yourself.

My mom was a very special lady. She never remarried in spite of a number of proposals. She told me how much she loved my dad, how he "rocked her socks," and how there was no one else like him. She wished aloud that I could have known him before the accident.

> *Tough times don't last, tough people do. The sun will rise and the stars will shine. A heart filled with hope has room for all good things.*

Virginia's little black book is among the most important things I've ever had. I look through it regularly. Turning to any page, I'm with her again. Of her 55 entries, there is not one she didn't live as part of her life.

Good Cop, Bad Cop

Rick DeSouza on his mother, Ida DeSouza

When I was entering fifth grade, I was placed in the accelerated academic class with Mrs. Reba Hoffman, who had a reputation of being the toughest teacher in our school. Worse yet, if you were in her fifth-grade class and passed, you would be placed in her sixth-grade class the next year.

After a week or so of some of the hardest work I had yet encountered, including learning French, I went to my mom to plead my case.

"Mom," I explained. "Mrs. Hoffman is too tough for me, and I shouldn't be in her class. All the kids are big brains and remember, I skipped that half year before fourth grade. I just don't belong in this group."

The next day we went to school together to meet with Mrs. Hoffman. When Mom explained the situation, Mrs. Hoffman said, "Mrs. DeSouza, Eric definitely belongs in this group. He just needs to apply himself a little more and then we will all see the results."

Despite my protests, Mom stood strong and agreed with my teacher. She made me stick it out.

At the time I thought my mom was being too demanding and unrelenting. But years later, I still tell anyone who will listen that Mrs. Hoffman was the best teacher that I ever had. She pushed me to work harder than I ever thought I could, and to do more things than I thought I was capable of. If not for Mom pushing me to be my best, I would have missed out on an experience that turned out to be an opportunity to learn and grow.

As an adult, I appreciate having learned that working hard and pushing yourself out of your comfort zone is important. It helped me keep my nose to the grindstone, to become a successful realtor, achieve athletic goals, and push for high standards of achievement for my own children.

Be All That You Can Be

June Howard on her mother, Laura Posey

I grew up on a farm in Tennessee. My mother's dream was for my sister and me to go to college. It was something that she had wanted for herself, but never had the opportunity. My mother's father died when she was 14, and my grandmother struggled to support the family after his death. In those days, and especially in the South, women were not encouraged to go to college. It was believed you should find a husband and spend your days in the home, cooking, cleaning, and caring for children. When my parents were married right after high school, my mom did have a job outside the home. However, she left it shortly after I was born to care for me and, a little later, my sister.

Every day after school we were required to practice piano for 30 minutes. When you are in third grade, 30 minutes is a long time. I still remember staring at the clock willing it to move faster! When I reached middle school, I decided to quit piano. I was tired of Bach and ready to do something more meaningful, like cheerleading. However, my mother had other plans. I did not quit—in fact I went on to take lessons through college, a total of 14 years on piano and organ.

I cannot tell you how grateful I am that I kept going. I have met so many people who quit and are sorry they did. Piano lessons taught me that I couldn't quit something just because it gets a little difficult. This persistence has been so important throughout my career and especially in my current role. When I lead major projects, I always run into a few obstacles that seem insurmountable; yet, as I reflect on those piano lessons, I somehow find the will to push forward to the finish.

I fulfilled my mother's dream in December 1988, when I became the first person in my family to graduate from college. My sister graduated in 1992 and became the first person in our family to receive a master's degree. My mom's dream continues with her grandchildren—my son and nephew are both in college now. Dreams do come true.

Work Isn't Work if You Love What You Do

Alanna Steffen-Nelson on her mother,
Erika Steffen

When I was in elementary school, I had trouble learning to read. I struggled and struggled and started doing everything I could to avoid what, increasingly, seemed like the task of reading. My mother believed that something was wrong, despite others telling her I was fine. She eventually was able to arrange for an expert consultation. The result? I was diagnosed with dyslexia.

My mother never let me use dyslexia as a reason to underachieve. She pushed me harder, instilled the same drive in me that she taught my brothers, and was always there to cheer me on. Her signature joyous "whoop-whoop" cheering was always embarrassingly loud for me, but it was filled with undeniable pride and joy. In school, for each hour my friends would study, I would have to study two to three hours just to gain the same knowledge. I would be discouraged, but she taught me to concentrate and push through. I developed new and different learning techniques. I learned to ask people for help when I needed it. Each time someone made fun of me or told me I couldn't do it, I worked harder and was more determined to prove them wrong.

All that hard work, combined with my mother's support and high expectations for me, paid very big personal dividends. The biggest was self-confidence and the ability to persevere through difficult things, which proved helpful when I was in graduate school completing my PhD. I learned to never give up on my goals or myself.

Mom Taught Me the Score

Howard Prager on his mother,
Sally Prager

My dad always amazed me because he was so successful in sales but had no interest in or knowledge of sports. So how did I become a sports fan? My mom.

My grandfather was an immigrant who worked seven days a week. So my mom, who was an only child, saw her uncles as role models. They were all baseball fans and took her to games. But my mom was not just a fan—when she grew up, she became a sportswriter. She wrote a series of baseball articles in the late 1940s for a barbershop journal. However, not wanting to reveal that she was a girl who knew baseball, she wrote under the pseudonym Lee Davis.

Later, Mom taught me how to play tennis and yelled "home run" when I hit the ball over the fence. She has always been an active player, even outside the sports arena—from being an election judge to sending my sister to one of the first integrated schools in Evanston, Illinois.

Sure I learned about sports, but she taught me so much more about the real score.

Inner Strength

Deja Perez on her mother, Haydee Gonzalez

My mom is the definition of gentle kindness. She always created a loving household and wanted people to feel warm and welcome. The rule in our house was that the first time you visit, we offered you drinks and food, but after that you were family.

When my mom was in school she wanted to be a psychiatrist. But I think she realized that she was too sensitive to take on everyone else's burdens. Then life happened—she moved to New Jersey from Puerto Rico and was never able to complete her degree.

I went through a "rough patch" between the ages of 14 and 16 and am probably responsible for a significant amount of my parents' gray hair. I was horrible to my mom for about a year and a half as I tried to express my independence. I purposely shut her out. But despite my attitude and mood swings, she never stopped loving me and trying to show me compassion.

When it came time to go to college, I wanted to make my parents proud. The day I graduated from college was so special. I could see how happy it made my mom. Although she never really talked about her own school years, I knew she wished she'd followed through with her education. Even so, she never swayed or pressured me to pursue a specific career path. My mom's lessons have been unconditional love, compassion, kindness, and gentleness; she has shown me the inner strength that at times we forget.

4

Being Courageous

"Success is not final, failure is not fatal; it
is the courage to continue that counts."
—Winston Churchill

Were it not for the protection that mothers provide, the world could seem like an overwhelmingly dangerous place. There are times in our lives when we need to face our fears—the fear of being an outcast, shunned, or punished for what we believe. We gain mental strength and moral determination by watching the actions of our mothers in the face of resentment or danger. When we see them respond with moral courage, resisting injustice or persevering in the face of hard times, we see courage in its fullest form.

Strong leaders demonstrate courage. They don't shy away from what needs to be said or done, and they let people know by word and deed where they stand. This isn't always easy. It's hard to face being reprimanded or criticized. Leaders with courage take the lead in facing up to problems, whether caused by people or unexpected crises, and act decisively and quickly to handle any issues.

In the stories that follow, you will read how mothers have demonstrated their courage against illness, age, discrimination, and economic circumstances. One thing they have in common is their will to succeed for themselves and for their children. They faced great difficulties and kept going, just as good leaders do.

The Power of Defiance

*Chad Merritt on his
mother, Mary Merritt*

I remember it well. We were at the mall on some errand. My mother, focused on her objective and corralling three children, took long strides while pushing a stroller. As we walked out of a department store and into the mall, I played my usual game of trying to step directly on the bricks while not touching the cracks. My younger sister, meanwhile, stared around at all the sights.

In the midst of my game, I looked up and realized my mother had that look on her face. She wasn't angry at me thankfully, but I knew she was angry. Her pace picked up a bit and she shook her head. A couple minutes later, I noticed her make eye contact with someone and stare right through them. Actually, it was a glare, a look of disdain; a look that said, "Say something, I dare you."

The woman on the receiving end of that glare quickly looked away, deciding she had business on the other side of the mall. But as she turned away from my mother, she glanced down at the original object of her attention—the stroller, the stroller where my foster brother sat napping.

For me, it was nothing to wake up one morning and have a new child in the house. I think T was around my 50th foster sibling. I was two when I found out that my brother and I were adopted, and what that meant: We had been born to other people, but our parents had loved us enough to select us; the connections of love and willingness trumped blood and bone. And through our fostering and the adoption of my sister, I knew that some children were born to families that weren't willing or able or healthy enough to raise children.

T stayed with us for well over a year. He had cerebral palsy, which made placement more complicated, and finding an adoptive family took more time. But his CP wasn't what made that woman stare—it wasn't noticeable at a glance as he was sleeping in a stroller.

No, my 10-year-old mind realized that the stare was because of his skin color. My mother was walking through the mall with a dark-haired son on one side, a blonde daughter on the other, and an African American baby in the stroller. To me, the situation was no different than other times we'd walked with other children. But for the first time, I saw that to others, it could have a different meaning. In their eyes, in their context, they filled in their perception with a different story that made my mother strange, different, and wrong.

As I looked up, my mother kept walking, making sure my sister and I were on either side of her, and our day went on. She never commented, never mentioned the incident or the others that followed. She may never have even realized that I was aware of the wordless exchanges. She didn't yell, she didn't argue, she simply stared them down with a defiant glare that challenged their racism. I learned that sometimes it's enough to hold your head up high, stare them down, and move on to the important things.

And that defiant glare, that focused, forceful walk, taught me in the moment that standing up to wrongness is never wrong.

Work Hard, Hold Your Head High, and Never Give Up!

Jay Glasscock on his mother, Anne Glasscock

My mom grew up in a loving family, but she had a tough upbringing with a strict mother and a father who suffered from alcoholism. Her mom and dad worked at the local textile mill, and the family did not have much in the way of material things.

Once Mom had to wear clothes made from a fabric that depicted old airplanes—definitely not what a young girl would want to wear. But they had to use what was available, and the fabric had been a gift during the war, so all three kids were made outfits from the same fabric. While my mom was embarrassed, she wore that outfit with pride, making it special by adding a yellow bow in her hair. The impressions she made on others were always important to her, and she soon began babysitting in her neighborhood and later waiting tables so she could buy a few nice things.

Mom worked hard in school, went to the local college, Winthrop University, and became a teacher. She met my dad and helped him through college after his tour of duty with the coast guard. Soon after his graduation, my brother and I were born, and Mom started the next chapter of her life as a teacher and mother.

Early on, my mom constantly reinforced the basic lesson of good manners and treating everyone with respect. She taught us to love all people, rich or poor, black or white, whatever religion. All people deserved our love, compassion, and most importantly respect.

Shortly after graduating from college, I came out as a gay man to my parents. They both grew up in religious homes in the South and were devout Christians. I was a bit nervous and concerned about how they would deal with my news. I had heard some folks at church comment on the unforgivable sin of being gay, and I knew my mom had always wanted grandchildren. However, my parents were amazing. Instead of reacting negatively, my mom said, "God made you who you are, people will judge you, but only God can judge your being, character, and deeds." They said they felt fortunate to have me as their son and that, while I should be careful, it did not change my potential in life or their love for me.

This lesson of being true to yourself and staying positive has served me well in all aspects of my life.

The Day My Mother Shocked Me

Neal R. Goodman on his mother,
Beatrice Gering Goodman

My mother was a white, working-class, Jewish Republican who believed strongly that staying in line, going to college, and doing my service in the army was the path I needed to take to move beyond my working-class background. I was her hopes and dreams. You can imagine her surprise when, as a high school junior, I became an activist and the leader of a civil rights campaign in my community and high school.

It was 1963, and this was her worst nightmare. She thought I might get "into trouble." I proposed that we address the issue of racism in the high school with our principal. He said he would consider allowing a two-minute opening inspirational presentation at an assembly in honor of "brotherhood." His idea of "brotherhood" was to do a letter exchange with students in Sweden. When I met with the principal to get approval for my opening comments and poem, he read my comments and told me I was a trouble maker and he was going to suspend me.

He called my mother to let her know what had happened. As I waited in the principal's office for my mother to arrive, all I could think about was how her dreams were going to be shattered when I was suspended. It was one of the longest hours of my life. When she came in, the principal handed her my "subversive" comments. She read them and told him that my comments and poem were exactly consistent with our country's values. A leader in the local veterans' association, she remarked that the friends of hers who went to fight in World War II and did not return had served so that we could live in a country that valued all peoples' rights. She threatened to take my case to the newspapers, hire an attorney, and get the local veterans' group leaders to go to the board of education to fight for me. My principal told her that he would give me another chance and let me create a brotherhood committee as part of the student council, as long as we limited our actions to his ideas of brotherhood.

My mother's actions that day truly shocked me. I went on to lead many civil rights activities in my community (although not in school) and, later in life, I became a professor of intercultural relations. I also started a company that became a leader in promoting diversity and inclusion in Fortune 1000 companies globally.

Make Light of the Unspeakable

Chuck Burak on his mother, Esther Burak

My mother lost her entire family—siblings and parents—in the Holocaust to the Nazis. Somehow, she survived, met my dad, who was also a Holocaust survivor, and gave birth to my older brother and me. When I was growing up, my mom never spoke about her experiences. It wasn't until I became an adult that she finally began to open up.

With her undaunted sense of humor, she could make light of the unspeakable. When people asked about the numbers burned into her forearm, she would (with a twinkle in her eye) say it was her phone number. Even with all that had happened to her and her family, my mom never spoke negatively or showed any kind of hatred. She would only share her experiences of the "good" days, the ones when she wasn't beaten or yelled at. Until her dying day in 2005, she never spoke of the Holocaust in a hateful or vengeful way. She truly taught me the extreme meaning of forgiveness.

My mother's experiences pushed me to be a leader I was proud to be. By example, she taught me to be positive, even in the most stressful of work experiences. She taught me to treat all people equally and to be the best listener and counselor I could be when helping people solve problems.

A Leg Up
on Me

Sharon Dobin Ross on her mother, Celia Dobin

At the age of 80, my mom was still running a dry goods store. One evening in the mid-1990s (March 3, Social Security check day), as she was leaving a doctor's office, she was mugged. The injuries to her eye were so bad that she was rushed from one hospital to another to try to save her vision, but she lost sight in her eye anyway. Unfortunately, no one noticed the abrasive sore on her left leg and it went untreated. Months later, her leg had to be amputated. My mom—that resilient, forward-thinking, 80-year-old woman who had direct deposit for her Social Security check and ran her own business—still ended up being an easy target for the mugger.

My mom's whole life changed in a flash. She sold the business and moved to an assisted care facility where she spent most of her days in a wheelchair. I trained the aides how to fit Mom with her artificial leg. A year later, her second granddaughter was getting married and my mom wanted to walk down the aisle. I helped her practice walking; it was very difficult for her. But she had grit, courage, and pride, and she was determined not to go down the aisle in a wheelchair.

On the day of the wedding, I took her to the back of the temple and helped her stand as she took the arm of my nephew. The two of them slowly made their way down the aisle, and I met her at the first row with her chair. That day my mom was inspirational to all who witnessed her getting one leg up on all of us.

Facing the Impossible

Sara Beth Schneider on her mother,
Mary Grace Melick

I always knew I had a pretty amazing mom. She was an entrepreneur who started her own business. Then, when I was in elementary school, my mom sold her business and began working with teenage mothers in an inner-city high school. When the school my brothers and I attended no longer fit our needs, she started a school to give us the kind of education many kids can only dream of. In the midst of all of this, she taught me lessons from her own life, listened to my problems, advised me, and showed me what it means to be a friend, wife, mother, sister, daughter, and businesswoman.

There were countless times where I would come home overwhelmed by a project or a situation and say, "I don't think I can do this." My mom would look at me and say, "Yes, you can. What steps do you need to take to make it happen?"

Because of this question, I spent two lunches a week with my math teacher reviewing homework to make sure I understood the concept. Because of this question, I learned to listen to another person's perspective and work with them to overcome our differences. Because of this question, when seemingly insurmountable problems came my way, I took a deep breath and made my plan for how to conquer them, one step at a time. I learned to push myself, to go beyond what I thought was my best and do what I thought was impossible.

In 2012, my mom was on her way to visit her brother when she was hit by a drunk driver. Against all odds, she survived the car accident, a coma, many abdominal injuries, a shattered pelvis, and much more. Suddenly, our roles switched: I became the caretaker for the woman who had always taken care of me. It was time for me to put everything I had learned from her into practice. As she recovered, I remembered the grace and dignity she exemplified so well, and I strove to return that to her even in her weakest moments. While it went against everything I wanted to do, I made my mom try to do things for herself. If she failed, I would step in. But more often than not, she was able to accomplish the things she thought was impossible, whether it was putting on her socks or learning to walk again.

As I've watched my mom recover, she shows me that very few things are impossible. She encourages me to take risks and make the hard choices. Through her, I am learning to be brave in my work, in my relationships, in my attitude, and in my choices. Because of my mom, I know that I can face the impossible.

Not Stepping Aside

Lynne De Lay on her mother,
Mildred A. De Lay

My mother was an unusual woman for her generation—especially in the South. As an only child and daughter, she was raised on a farm in Georgia, blending traditional male and female roles by working alongside her father in tasks that would have been done by her brothers—if she had had any. She learned early on how to do hard work without complaining.

In World War II she became a draftsman with the Tennessee Valley Authority (TVA), and was soon working alongside the men in that capacity even when they returned home. I grew up watching my mother balancing two roles: taking care of the house (she was gifted with a needle and a terrific cook) and watching her work at the drafting table with all the accoutrements as a draftsman.

She was asked to leave TVA shortly after she married my father. He also worked there, and the rules didn't allow a husband and wife to work in the same organization. Like other women who were working traditionally male-dominated roles, she was asked to "step aside" because it was important to accommodate the men who were returning from the war. Not letting that stop her, my mother went on to work under contract with several organizations who needed drafting work done.

Toward the middle of her career, my mother was again asked to step aside, but in a different way. Over the years, she transitioned from external contractor to company employee. When the manager of her department retired, my mother applied for his job. In the interview, she was told that while she may have been the most qualified, they could not promote her because the men just would not work for a woman. Seeing the futility of fighting the system in the early 1960s in the South, she transitioned out of that department and created a whole new role for herself in the company. This set her up for another transition into real estate, where she became a member of the million-dollar club (in sales) and a state office holder with the Tennessee Realtors Association. Obstacles or difficulties were simply challenges to be met head-on with a smile.

Mother never took a leadership course, but "modeling the way" seemed to come naturally. As her daughter, I learned the value of hard work, determination, of doing my best, having high expectations and standards, and a desire to continually learn and grow. Mother could negotiate with the best of the men and it was not uncommon for the men, after negotiating with her, to come away fatigued and with an increased respect for her abilities. She was a Southern woman who defied the stereotype and engaged with men as their equal while still dressing elegantly as a woman. As her daughter, I was sometimes embarrassed by her more assertive or courageous tendencies. Deference was not her strong suit, yet she was always respectful.

Mother encouraged me to chart my own independent path—to not be a mindless follower of the crowd or tradition. She encouraged me to stretch myself, garner any learning, and go after what I wanted.

Once at the local theater I played the lead female role in a major play. After the opening night performance, the director told me what a good job I had done, and that I had exceeded his expectations. The rest of the cast and those from the audience who came backstage were complimentary, too. I felt good. When I returned home, I wanted my mother's thoughts. She was both my biggest advocate and my worst critic. I liked all the praise I'd received, but it felt incomplete. So, I asked my mother, "OK, how did I really do?" True to form, she outlined the positive and how, if I were to do it again, I might still improve. Such was our relationship.

Might Sometimes Comes in Small Packages!

David Turner on his mother, Esther Turner

My mother was quite attractive, and once when she was younger she was asked out by a good-looking guy with a bad reputation. He was into cars and hung with a fast crowd. So, she brought a six-inch hatpin on their first date and made sure he knew she had it. I guess she figured it would help her get the degree of respect she expected from him. She didn't need it! He fell in love with her without the need or encouragement of a hatpin, and they were together for more than 55 years. They showed each other, and their children, love and respect. I attribute my long, happy marriage to their example.

Depression tormented my mother for most of her adult life. But she never hid it, despite the stigma attached to that disease. The depression made it difficult for her to appear strong and sometimes she failed; however, she showed a lot of fortitude in dealing with things she couldn't control.

My mother didn't mind if you thought she was weak or timid. In fact, she preferred it. She didn't need to prove she could do something, and she would rather let others do the hard work. When she had to do the heavy lifting though, she would step up and get it done. My mother valued respect. She gave it as well as expected it. She always gave someone respect until they showed they weren't deserving of it. My father showed me how to be a man, but my mother made sure he did it the right way.

Appreciation

Lew Stern on his mother, Marilyn Stern Rice

My mom was diagnosed with breast cancer in 1963. I remember the day I came home from middle school to find that she had gone to the hospital for her first surgery. I didn't know if she'd be coming back. When she came home a week later, I found her in the living room laughing with friends, making sure everyone else was OK. For the next 31 years she went through many different treatments, but her cancer kept coming back, eventually spreading to her ribs, lungs, and spine.

She never complained. She survived—she was more than her cancer. She always focused on what she could do for everyone else. She woke up with a smile, appreciating the new day and what she had.

My mom's compassion for everyone she touched over her 69 years changed them for the better. Her energy was contagious. My parents wrote musical comedies together and would direct them all around Boston—at the VA hospital, for the disabled, and for anyone who wouldn't otherwise experience the arts. They also raised money for music scholarships for college students in need of financial help. At 45, Mom went to college and grad school to get degrees in special education. She then taught elementary school and piano.

We're all affected by the emotions of those around us every day. No matter what was going on in her life, my mom always shared positive emotions and a deep and sincere interest in everyone's life. She profoundly influenced the way we live, our confidence, and our focus on others.

You Have to

Persevere in Life

———

Mark Bocianski on his mother, Doreen Bocianski

———

My mom always told me that "You have to persevere in life."

Born in Liverpool on January 31, 1922, Doreen May Kelly was the oldest of three children. When she was 17, Britain and France declared war on Germany, and life as my mother knew it was about to change. Her family built an air raid shelter in the backyard, and after finishing high school she started working for the Automatic Telephone service.

My mother was quite adventurous. To help with the war effort, she became an airplane spotter looking for enemy planes. She was stationed atop a tall building and had to slide down a zipline when the air raid alarm sounded. During the bombing of Liverpool, her family would spend the entire night in their shelter. Each morning, she and her family started working or taking care of the garden, as if bombings were routine.

After my mother got married, she moved to the United States because my father's family lived in Chicago. She worked part time until my parents separated when I was 11; then she worked full time to make ends meet. She rarely missed a day's work. She would take the bus, even in the bitter cold and heavy snow. Once she fell and hurt her ankle badly. She simply bandaged it up and went to work the next day as if nothing happened. In retail, you stand all day.

My mother modeled a very strong work ethic that defined my work ethic and that of my children. When I first started working after college and had a day off, she would ask me if that was OK with my employer. If I left early for an appointment she would question why I was home early. To this day, she still asks me if it is OK to take a day off. She recently turned 95, and I take her to the mall once a week where she shops with her walker for a few hours. If I try to help her in or out of the car, she says she must do it herself. She will say, "You know you have to persevere in life."

5

Integrating Resolve
With Humility

"Great leaders don't need to act tough.
Their confidence and humility serve
to underscore their toughness."
—Simon Sinek

From the time mothers get up in the morning until they go to sleep at night, they multitask to do all the work needed for their families. They do this to provide for their families, support their colleagues at work, and help their communities without expecting great accolades. Children depend on their mothers' perseverance and fierce resolve to create a safe and nurturing world for them. Often moms go on resolutely in spite of challenging circumstances. There are tough times in everyone's life—seeing how our mothers face challenges and persevere teaches us how to do so as well. It builds our confidence. Their determination and confidence often determines success or failure.

In his book *Good to Great,* Jim Collins called the combination of genuine personal humility with fierce resolve Level 5 Leadership. These behaviors build strong families and strong organizations. In our work with leaders, they have often shared stories about how seeing their mothers demonstrate these behaviors shaped their current approach to leadership.

Find the Broom

*Susannah McMonagle on her
mother, Candy Cobb*

The saying *find the broom* means that when your work or responsibilities end—you find the broom. You sweep the floors. Wipe down the coffee counter. Send an uplifting email to a colleague. Help a co-worker finish a PowerPoint deck. Spend an extra hour showing clients around town. Thank the concierge or valet with an extra tip. Pick up your husband's shoes for the 1,000th time. You find the broom. And, you do it without being asked or expecting your action to be noticed. My mother exemplifies this philosophy more than anyone I've ever known.

In high school, I made the varsity volleyball team as a freshman. However, as the most junior person on the team, I was forced to carry heavy bags of balls, fill water bottles, and load uniforms in the laundry; all the remedial things that underclassman are often forced to do as a "rite of passage." When I complained to my mom, she said "buck up." Then she had the nerve to suggest that I use the proper washer and dryer settings when I washed all the stinky uniforms. Find the broom.

As I got older, I watched her walk the talk. At my wedding, she handled every detail, mishap, and guest with absolute grace. She made centerpieces, signs, decorations, and brunch tickets. She stayed up late and got up early, not just because of these specific tasks, but because finishing one job simply meant finding the broom.

When I think about my mom as my first coach, I can't imagine a better lesson—not just because finding the broom is a great mindset for life, but because the small, often unnoticed actions are the ones that make other people's lives better too.

I'm a Poker

John Betof on his mother, Jean Seeger Betof

I had flown in from Arizona to Cranbury, New Jersey, to be with my mom on her 75th birthday. During breakfast she said that she would like to take a drive to see the Barnegat Lighthouse on the northern tip of Long Beach Island in Ocean County. It would take us about an hour and a half to get there by car. I had never been to the lighthouse, and I could tell that she really wanted to go, so the two of us piled in my rental car and got on the road.

As we arrived, I was struck by how tall the lighthouse was. Mom said to me, "We're climbing to the top." I asked her if she was up to climbing the requisite 217 steps. With conviction in her voice, she said, "Let's get going." I followed her as we began climbing. After a little while, when Mom stopped to catch her breath she said to me, "I'm a poker; I may be slow, but I'm persistent, and I'll get to the top." When we finally made it to the top, Mom was so proud of herself for accomplishing what she set out to do at breakfast that day.

I often reflect on what she said to me at Barnegat Lighthouse that day. Mom wasn't out to impress me by how quickly she could climb those lighthouse steps; instead, she "poked" her way up one step at a time. Her tenacity and persistence in whatever she undertook has always been inspiring to me. I often say to people when I'm hiking or mountain biking, "I'm a poker. Go ahead and pass me." Now that I'm older I may not be fast, but I'm still persistent. I'll get to wherever I'm going in work and in life.

Crossed Every Bridge but One

Lisa Mathis on her mother, June Payne

My mother always said, "Lisa, I have crossed every bridge but one." I was so confused by this statement. My parents divorced when I was 14 years old. Afterward, my mother served as mother, father, disciplinarian, teacher, supporter, spiritual adviser, coach, and cheerleader; she worked two jobs—sometimes three. Being my best friend was not an option for her: "I am your mother," she would say, and that was that.

But a bridge? What does that really mean? I often asked myself that question. A bridge can be defined in so many ways, and the structures are vast and different. To her, the bridges were challenges, and she would later teach me these lessons.

The first bridge is pride: Always be proud of who you are. Look up and speak up, maintain eye contact with people, and smile. Smile and the world smiles with you. Don't ever let people tell you what you can't do. Persevere with pride and dignity.

The second bridge is common people. What does this even mean? My mother always said, "Common people are just common, and they have nothing to offer. Surround yourself with positive people who want to make something out of themselves and who share the same values as you do." In her mind, a "common person" wasn't ambitious. They had no goals. They couldn't see the future and they wanted to remain where they were. Don't surround yourself with common people.

The third bridge is adversity: After my parents divorced, we experienced pain, sorrow, and definite setbacks, but my mother demonstrated resilience and had faith. She always said, "Get your act together and your mind right and you will prevail."

The fourth bridge is risk taking: Be disciplined and finish what you start. Travel the world, read everything—even subjects that bore you. Make sure you take care of your health and always stretch yourself; you need to be afraid—"real" afraid—to grow to greatness. And by the way, don't let boys distract or scare you. (I have two brothers and she was right!)

The fifth bridge is to look the part: Image is everything. My mother was an excellent seamstress. In the early 1960s she worked at a factory sewing clothes. When she came home she would make dinner and sew a pretty dress for me. I was the best-dressed child in kindergarten. She taught me to always look the part and dress the part no matter where you are going, because first impressions mean a lot and image is everything.

It's Not by Magic

Donna McNamara and Winni McNamara on
their mother, Bella McNamara

Our mother was a determined person. When she decided on a goal, she applied herself with commitment and constancy of purpose. Mom didn't rely on good luck or chance. She knew that it's not by magic that things get done; it's by hard work and dedication.

Early on, Mom's spirit and strong will were the fabric of exciting stories of her young adulthood. She grew up in a sheltered family environment during the Depression, living with her parents, older brother, and twin sisters on a dairy farm in a small Portuguese community in Massachusetts. But once Mom finished high school, she decided to step out on her own. Unusual for the times and for how she was brought up, Mom stretched her own mother's limits and eventually made the bold decision to move to Washington, D.C., and become a working woman.

As we were getting older and preparing to leave home, Mom decided it was time for another big change in her life. Partially motivated by the cost of our college educations, she set her sights on becoming a nurse, a formidable goal for someone who had not been in school for almost 30 years. At first it was awkward to watch her study, struggle, and work hard to pass tests. But later we watched her graduate and wear her starched white uniform and nurse's cap with confidence and distinction.

When she was 55, our mom decided to learn to downhill ski. Her single-minded focus was surprising, and her approach was definitely unusual. She had never been an athlete or lived near mountains, so she chose a particularly unique skiing technique—she snowplowed her way down the entire length of even the longest runs. If you know anything about skiing, you can understand that this was a daunting task.

As her daughters, we see what a powerful example she set for us as she took on a very difficult challenge, and through determination and grit persisted until it was accomplished.

What's Really Important in Life

Ted Kauffman on his mother, Ann Sklersky

My mom taught me what was really important in life—respect, humility, kindness, hard work, resilience, and honesty. These values are taught by our parents' actions, not their words.

I grew up watching my mom live those values. For her it meant rising every morning at five to work as a seamstress in a factory or volunteering to sew clothing for an old age home. She even donated her life savings to Israel during the Six-Day War.

These values help me get through difficult situations in my professional life. My business partner and I have been close to bankruptcy a few times. When you are in this type of situation—when payrolls are cut, people are terminated, and severe changes are made—everyone who works for you is focused on your actions. If you don't handle the situation with respect, honesty, and humility, you will lose everyone's trust. If you handle it with the values you learned from your mother, you not only survive; you become more successful and your company gets stronger.

The Privilege of Work

Ronni Goodman Ozello on her mother,
Florence Goodman

My mother never regarded work as a hardship or a task to be avoided. Work was a way to make the money necessary to survive and it was always deemed a privilege. During the Depression, my mother quit high school to work in a factory to help support her parents and five siblings. She worked a long day and her paycheck was a small but necessary reward.

My father, who worked until he joined the army during World War II, shared her enthusiasm for work. My parents never earned enough to live above the paycheck to paycheck level. My father lost a business when I was in high school, and he then suffered a series of heart attacks. It was devastating. How would the bills get paid? How would their two girls get a college education? My resilient mother found a factory job making dancing costumes. My father died at 51, and my mother continued working until her early 70s. Money was always a worry, a lifelong stress, but work was never too hard or too much of a task. It was never something to be avoided.

My sister and I have worked most of our adult lives. We, too, regard work as a great privilege. We both achieved advanced college degrees with scholarships and loans. Thanks to the work ethic we inherited from our parents, we both found good jobs and more financial security than our parents ever had.

Persistent Mom

Lisa MD Owens on her mother,
Delores Donnelly

When I was in college, I drove home for some family time one
fall weekend. I wore my favorite gold Georgia Tech jacket to
keep the chill off. Mom, as always, greeted me at the door with
a kiss and a hug: "Welcome home, dear." Then, as I passed her
and headed toward the kitchen, she asked, "What is that black
stuff on your jacket?"

I took off the jacket and looked. It was covered in tiny black
letters. Oh no! Just before I drove home, I'd toured the Georgia Tech print room where the school newspaper was printed.
I must have leaned up against something with printer ink all
over it. My jacket was ruined!

"Do you want to try to clean it?" Mom asked. I spent 10
minutes scrubbing with Comet cleaner and hot water. Nothing

worked. I came out of the laundry room and plunked down on the couch, dejected and upset.

"Let me get the casserole in the oven, then I'll see if I can get the stain out," Mom said. I just grumped. "Nothing will work, Mom. It's INK!" But she went into the laundry room anyway to give it a go. Twenty minutes later, she came out and showed me a six-inch section that she'd cleaned.

"If I use Dad's hand cleaner and a scrub brush, I'm getting it out. It's a slow job, but it seems to be working," she said. It was working! "So," she asked, "would you like to take over and finish cleaning it?"

"Mom! It took you 20 minutes to clean a small part of the entire back side of the jacket. It'll take hours to do the entire thing," I said with a defeated attitude. "It's just a loss. It can't be done."

"OK," she said.

The next morning, there, hanging on the back of my chair at the kitchen table, was my gold jacket, free of ink. She'd stayed up all night to finish cleaning it. Of course she got a big hug and many thanks. But the real thanks came over the years that followed. Whenever I ran into a big problem, one that felt insurmountable, I thought back to my mom and my jacket.

She taught me that as long as I start on a part of the problem, and then keep working at it, I can succeed.

6

Innovating While Leading

"If you always do what you always did, you
will always get what you always got."
—Unknown

Leaders of many types of organizations, such as businesses, not-for-profit organizations, government agencies, schools, and sports teams face, a common challenge. To be successful in the short and long term, they must innovate. Continuous improvement and breakthrough thinking only happen when innovation is fostered by leaders.

Most high-performing organizations are characterized by leaders who are constantly driving innovation. These leaders consistently model and encourage a culture of experimentation, trust building, teamwork, and risk taking. They also believe that personal accountability is vital for innovation to occur. When we asked leaders how they learned or experienced innovation practices, we frequently heard stories about their childhood and how they were raised.

Moms innovate all the time. It comes with the territory. They often have a plan for the day or week. Then "stuff" happens. Mothers feel accountable for keeping it all together while juggling all the other aspects of their lives. They experiment and find new solutions to both predictable and unpredictable challenges. Mothers help build trust and teamwork within their families. They also teach their children how to take reasonable risks while ensuring the necessary security at home.

Word Presents

Jennifer Finkelstein on her mother, Patti Isakov

My mother was generous with her jewelry and would let my sister and me try on some of her pieces. During services or quiet ceremonies, she made a game out of putting a fancy ring or two on our fingers. We loved the sparkle. One day when I was small, she let me wear a piece of jewelry to a party—a lovely whistle on a chain. It was an antique. I ran around outside with pure glee, until—as I'm sure you've guessed—I lost it.

My mother wasn't angry, although certainly she was upset. In that moment she taught me how to talk openly about disappointments and losses. I guess it's no surprise that I am a psychotherapist today. One could say, I've been practicing for years.

My mother often gave word presents—the gift of a compliment, a positive statement, or an acknowledgment. Thanks to her, I never hesitate to give word presents to those I love.

Today her voice is still a balm on a bad day. And she knows by the sound of my hello how I'm really doing. I crave her voice because I know it will bring the kind of intimate conversation that goes deep effortlessly, when needed, and offers something medicinal beyond any superficial support others can give. And I am so grateful that I know how to do this kind of talking.

My Beloved Betty B

Jane Barr Horstman on her mother, Betty Barr

When I was 25, I managed a real estate investment company office and needed an "office girl." We hired numerous temps, but none of them could do the job well. When I told my boss that my mom could do a better job, he told me to hire her. So I did, and for the next six-and-a-half years, I was my mom's supervisor. She did not want me to call her mom at work, so I called her Betty and she signed all her notes to me as Betty B (although she was the only Betty in the office). Hence, my beloved Betty B was born.

She made my lunches and they were great; if she'd made roast beef the night before, there was always a sandwich for my lunch, as well as fruit and great dessert. One of the young men who worked in our office even offered to pay her $20 a day to bring his lunch, to which she replied that he was not one of her children and he should call his mother in Europe if he wanted lunch.

To paraphrase Ralph Waldo Emerson, Betty B succeeded in all the ways that matter. She laughed often and much; she won the respect of intelligent people and the affection of children; she found the best in others and she will leave the world a better place because she lived.

Spell Wednesday

Eunice Sevilla Nuyles on her
mother, Nona Sevilla

I was five when I learned how to spell Wednesday, and I was
also five when I learned the notion of "creative tension." One
may wonder how a kindergartner's brain could absorb both
basic and profound concepts, but my mom knew she couldn't
overengineer how to phase my learning. That's one of the perks
of being raised by a mom of nine. You learn what you learn
beyond your age.

One day Mama helped me learn how to spell Wednesday. She was so determined; I remember us going through
WED-NES-DAY a hundred times over. The next day in class I
chanted WED-NES-DAY secretly and quietly to myself. When
the teacher asked who could spell Wednesday, I was one of the
few who raised their hands confidently. I could feel excitement
building up; it felt like my entire body was shaking! I wanted so

much to show the entire class that I got this—that I was smart, I did my homework, and I could spell Wednesday. Another kid got called, and my heart sank. As she walked to the board to begin writing, I watched like a hawk. Aha! She missed a letter! There's hope, I thought, so I desperately raised my hand and this time got noticed. I walked toward the board, my heart pounding, silently chanting WED-NES-DAY in my mind. I wrote the word *Wednesday* with such ease and confidence. I can't recall what happened next; I just remember that it felt good, insanely good. That was my first taste of success, and my mom was the persistent coach behind it.

When I got home that afternoon, I couldn't wait to tell her what just happened—how excited I was as I walked to the front of the class, how my palms were sweaty, and how my knees felt like Jell-O. As expected, she praised me for being the smartest in class, but then she began explaining that the experience I described as I walked up to the board was called creative tension. It was that feeling of knowing—knowing you worked hard and prepared well for something and knowing you have the right answer, and now have the opportunity to share that "eureka" moment. Wow. Big phrase. I was five.

Fast forward to today. As a leader, I use creative tension to fuel my presentations, bring energy into my work, and bridge the gap between where I am now and where I want to be. Each time I prepare for something big or attend a meeting I deem challenging, I channel my nervousness back to that day I learned to spell Wednesday.

She Got the Project Started

Jerry Hurwitz on his mother, Marilyn Hurwitz

I worked my way through college as a house painter. One summer, my mother wanted her kitchen painted, but I was slow to plan this into my busy schedule. I always had an excuse—another job or commitment—that prevented me from putting her small kitchen into my schedule.

Then, one day I came home after work to find my mother, brush in hand, painting the kitchen on her own. She was making a mess of it, but she got the project started. She knew I would take over as soon as I walked in the door. Which, of course, is exactly what I did.

I have applied her lesson many times in my business career. Once when I was a plant manager, I wanted some cleaning and maintenance done in part of the plant that the maintenance workers never seemed to get to. They kept telling me they had more pressing problems to address. While that was probably true, one afternoon I decided to start the work on my own. After their initial amazement that a plant manager would actually do the work, my team jumped in and we worked together until the task was complete. Later we even had some good laughs over it.

Mom Saves the Day

Maribeth D. Renne on her mother,
Wilma Jean Ryan Dillon

My mother was a beautiful bookworm who grew up during the Depression in a family with seven children in a southwestern Pennsylvania coal mining town. Her father's employment as a carpenter and her mother's kitchen garden enabled them to do better than many other families, but things were still tough. She never went to college, but was still the smartest and most insightful woman I've ever known.

My dad nicknamed my mother the Queen of Make Do. She was more resilient than most. And it's a good thing because my sisters and I tested her resilience daily. I was scatterbrained, often forgetting to tell my mother about things I was required to take to school.

One morning, I was jolted awake by the sudden memory that I was supposed to take oyster crackers to school that day.

My teacher, a Catholic nun, wanted everyone to bring these specialty crackers to simulate communion wafers in our practice for receiving the sacrament of First Holy Communion.

Anxiously running down the stairs, I called out frantically to my mother. We were not a household that regularly stocked oyster crackers and, in those days, grocers did not open their doors until well after school started. The situation was dire; there was truly nothing I feared more than the wrath of Sister Herman Joseph.

I found my mother in the kitchen balancing two fussy babies, my twin sisters, on her lap. She calmly took in my overwrought state and somehow drew me in for a hug. Reminding me that it would have been nice if I had thought of the crackers the afternoon before, she urged me to eat my breakfast and then run upstairs to dress for school. I could see her mind going into action as she reassured me that she would think of a solution.

Nibbling on cinnamon toast, I watched as my mother moistened slices of Wonder Bread and then rolled them out flat. She reached for a shot glass, carefully cut around the base of the glass, and produced tiny disks that she lifted into the warm oven to dry. By the time I was ready for school, my mother had made a box of perfect communion wafers.

I was nervous as I carried my box into the classroom, eyeing my classmates with their oyster crackers and worrying that mine were not exactly what Sister Herman Joseph had instructed us to bring. She took one look at my contribution and displayed a rare smile. She was so impressed and pleased that my mother had spent the extra effort to produce perfect communion wafers for our class practice. Thanks to my mother, I was the shining star that day.

Midwestern Mom: Global Citizen

*Donna M. Beestman and Mary McDowell on
their mother, Ardith McDowell*

Our mother lived her 98 years with dignity, a zest for life, a sense of purpose, a commitment to family, a love of nature, and a keen interest in the people and cultures of her own communities and the world. Although she never lived more than 50 miles away from the small Wisconsin farm where she was born, she truly modeled what it is to be a citizen of the world and demonstrated what one committed person can do to contribute constructively to international goodwill. She did this by facilitating, in countless ways, the creation of thousands of person-to-person connections between Americans and people around the world.

Even though she was a busy mother of five, Mom reached out and welcomed many international university students into our home. There were often several additional guests from countries all over the world at the family dinner table on Thanksgiving Day or Easter. Ours was often the only American family those students got to know during their stay in the United States. The perspectives of our own family were greatly enriched by these early opportunities to meet individuals of other races, cultures, languages, and nationalities. Our mom would remark, "In a university town, the world can come to your door!"

In 1964—in the midst of the Cold War—Mom led one of the first groups of American women to visit the Soviet Union. While she was there, she insisted on attending a church service on Sunday morning. She and the group stood in the packed church, listening to the entire service and singing along in English. When the service ended, people in the congregation embraced her, pointing to their own hearts to convey that being together and sharing their common faith created a connection beyond the political differences of our two countries.

Our mother truly valued being a global citizen. She inspired many of her friends, children, and grandchildren to seek out international experiences, both personal and professional, to travel and learn about other cultures. It's a gift we have truly valued in our own lives.

You Have
Two Minutes

Jennifer Hanson Long on her mother,
Joan Hanson

We all have everyday complaints. My mom taught me that if you are going to complain you might as well make it entertaining. She also said to give it a time limit because while complaining never solves anything, sometimes you just have to let it out and you need someone you trust to listen. Here's what I mean.

I had a bad day at work—one of those "the world is against me" kind of days. So what do I do? I call my mom. She picks up the phone and says, "Hi, honey. How was your day?"

"Hi, Mama. Ughh. It was fine," I reply in a huffy tone.

"OK, you have two minutes."

I begin the epic tale of my bad day. "I spilled coffee on my blouse, and of course it was on the part that is white and not the blue part. My computer is slow and hates me, and then I found out some blue cord wasn't plugged in, which apparently is important. Words were hard today, and I fumbled through a meeting. I was tired all day, and I was imagining what it would look like if I took a nap in my cube and what people would say. My lunch tasted gross, and I knew I should have ordered the mac and cheese rather than the salad; meh . . . that's what I get for trying to be healthy I guess. And traffic was the worst, and I saw someone pick their nose."

"Uff, sounds like a day," Mom responds. "Thanks for making it entertaining."

"Thanks, Mom, for listening."

Mom, the CFO of Our Household

Molly D. Shepard on her mother, Nancy Shepard

My mother could have been a chief financial officer had she been born in a different time. A graduate of Smith College in 1942, she was expected to get married and raise happy and successful children. None of her friends went to work and, as she was engaged to be married by her senior year, her future as a wife and mother and soon the spouse of a naval officer was cemented.

But my mother was frustrated by not having an outlet or career for her intellect, leadership skills, and energy. So, she poured this energy into my father's career, her family, our home, and her community activities. The one time she entertained going to work, she was abruptly shut down by my father. He told her in no uncertain terms that his wife was not getting a job.

Mom managed all the finances for the family and her four kids, including all investments. Every afternoon she would sit at a small antique desk in the corner of our living room and spend an hour or two paying bills, speaking to her stock broker, and recording all the expenditures and stock purchases in ledger books in her funny large scroll. During these hours we were never allowed to interrupt her. She dispensed our allowances from this desk, always asking us to account for how we were going to spend the money. When we were older and ready, she gave us all lessons on how to manage our money and our family's money when we got married. As head of her investment club, she was proud of her portfolio, which outperformed all her peers' investments.

Mom had a few rules she followed and that she imparted to us:

- Always manage your own money and keep it in your name.
- Always pay your bills in full each month.
- Do not take on a mortgage or incur debt, ever!
- Live within your means!
- Invest wisely but do invest.

These were not always easy rules to follow, but I never forgot them. I've used them as guiding principles my whole life.

7

Managing Change

"It is not the strongest of the species that survives,
nor the most intelligent that survives. It is the
one that is the most adaptable to change."
—Charles Darwin

Growth within all people and organizations requires change. Every mother dreams that her children will grow up to be stable, well-functioning adults. To fulfill that dream, mothers must create the foundation of skills and values for their children from an early age. As teenagers, an idea begins to form about what their life will be like when they grow up. Mothers play a major role in preparing them for the challenges that lie ahead. At various points, children often resist what it takes to grow and change. Being more grown up means you have to go to school, do homework, study, practice an instrument, or do chores, all of which build accountability, strengthen values, and develop skills. At times, change can seem scary. Going to a new school and making new friends is hard. Moms are there to celebrate the incremental successes and provide comfort and support as children develop and change for the better, especially during the hard times.

Managing change is one of the critical skills leaders need to learn in their careers. Organizations, like people, are in a constant state of change. Leaders must be able to build the vision of what change will look like, why it is important to the success of the enterprise, and how to overcome any resistance to change. It is often said that people don't resist change; they resist being changed. So, leaders, like moms, need to learn how to initiate change and build the vision and momentum necessary for it to occur. Leaders, like moms, need to prepare the organization for the challenges ahead, address the fears about change, and celebrate the successes on the way to achieving important goals.

When Less Is More

Bob Levin on his mother, Ruth Levin

My mother was a doctor's daughter. Her father was a big *macher,* to use the Yiddish word, in a small Catskills town, and she idolized him. She even entertained thoughts of going to med school herself, but he steered her away. It's the only negative thing I ever heard her say about her father—although she said it wistfully, without rancor. Over the years she somehow transferred her idolatry of her dad to doctors in general, to the entire medical profession, which was a mixed blessing when I became seriously ill at the age of 18.

My parents sprang into action, whisking me home from college and into a hospital in Philadelphia where I was biopsied and diagnosed. My mother always insisted on having "the best man in the city"—a running joke between my brother and me. Now she and my father researched the best centers in the country for my type of cancer. They settled on Boston.

"When you treat one Levin you treat all Levins," she said to my new doctor, clutching his hands and gazing into his eyes. I was mortified, even insulted—I was the one who'd soon be barfing.

Conveniently, my brother lived in Boston at the time, so I stayed with him while getting daily doses of radiation at the hospital. But my parents also sublet a nearby apartment, where my mother fed me all of my favorite home-cooked meals. I was grateful for the food, but chafed at her unrelenting, watery-eyed gaze. Nor did I appreciate her constant morbid presence beside my hospital bed, reading her prayer book after my surgery.

I was a teenager and thus invincible, yet my mother's body language suggested otherwise. Who needed that, however well meaning? I told my friends that I was sure I'd beat cancer, but might die of my mother.

I returned to college that spring, even though I was still getting monthly chemo treatments. I'm amazed now that my parents allowed this, that they trusted a local doctor to give my injections and my friends to put me to bed and watch over me. In that early era of chemo—primitive by today's standards—I was mostly unconscious for the day after my treatments, only waking occasionally to vomit into an old pot.

That summer my girlfriend and I worked as counselors at a camp for inner-city kids. This was, in retrospect, insane—I was still driving back and forth from New Jersey to Boston for chemo. Depleted as I was, I oversaw a cabin full of unruly preteens, I ate and slept with them, and I led them on hikes and in ball games. No one tried to talk me out of this madness, not even my overprotective mom, who had obviously decided I needed my freedom—even the freedom to be foolish.

Years later, when my cancer returned, she wanted to come visit me in Toronto but kept her distance, letting my wife see me through treatment—administered, we assured her, by the best man in the city.

"I know it's harder for you when I'm there," she said, sighing into the phone.

I can imagine her praying, even consulting with her deceased dad, bargaining with him. It must have been wrenching for her, this restraint; yet she recognized the discomfort her anxiety caused me—and, in the process, allowed me to build confidence in my own ability to face down life's demons.

The Mixture Is Better

Marion Molineaux Feigenbaum on her mother,
Valentina (Nina) Solchaga de Molineaux

In 1955, Valentina Solchaga was a small Panamanian woman at a dance hall on a U.S. military base hoping to meet a young, American GI. She did. He was her complete opposite—tall, blue-eyed, very educated—but he loved to dance and spoke Spanish fluently. Later, his many love letters in Spanish convinced her to marry him and she came to New York as Nina Solchaga de Molineaux, bringing a halting knowledge of English and a love of all people and most of all food. Our home was tumultuous—I had four siblings, each about a year apart, and our relatives lived with us from time to time. We moved a lot and each neighborhood we lived in was a messy, complete melting pot. Speaking of pots, there was always a huge one on the stove—*arroz con pollo, pernil*—whatever we could make for a large crowd. Neighbors, my brothers' friends, and strangers always dropped by when Nina was cooking.

This made no sense to me. Unlike my siblings, who seemed to thrive on the noise and chaos, I was shy and always looking for a quiet place to hide. I asked my mother why she let everyone wander in and out of our house; why did it have to be so crazy? To which she responded:

"*Mi vida,* don't you know that '*la mezcla es mejor*'?" she responded. "The mixture is better." It makes for better-looking children, she laughed naughtily, having delicious food, friends from all over the world, and an education you can't get in school.

I didn't understand her then, but I sure do now. When I am with my four siblings and our families it is still complete chaos, but the children are beautiful and the food and laughter is everything. That little Panamanian mom of ours was so smart. *La mezcla es mejor*—always.

Lucile

Mark Morrow on his mother, Lucile Morrow

Like millions of other women of her generation, my mother waited patiently for my father to return from World War II and marry her. It's hard to imagine anyone today with such disciplined patience, but in 1944 my mother's courage of conviction was common, even expected, behavior. So, when my father returned from North Africa after nearly four years they were married within a week.

I would like to believe that my mom's faith in her true love's return cast a magical spell that protected my father throughout the war and allowed him to come home nearly unscathed. Still, even fervent prayers and magic are not enough to shield a soldier from all harm. Toward the end of the war, a German Messerschmitt spotted my father's jeep as it raced back to join his company after he'd called in artillery coordinates in advance of expected troop movements. The Messerschmitt filled his jeep full of holes and seriously wounded him. How one of the bullets that tore through his body that day did not kill him is an unanswerable mystery of life. Many soldiers fully recover from their war wounds and are grateful for their second chance at life. Others, like my father, never recover and are haunted the rest of their lives by the dark, indelible burden of worry and fear.

Despite my father's psychological wounds—his undiagnosed PTSD often made him angry and nearly always fearful and unable to act—he and my mom built a happy life together. Eventually, my father had a complete mental breakdown and was forced to leave his job. When my brother and I noticed our father not going to work anymore, our mom sat us down and told us that our father was "sick," and that she was going back to work and that, for now at least, our father would be staying home. No drama. She was doing what she had to do. Things were going to change and that was it.

She got a job as a bookkeeper at a local drugstore and in doing so discovered a competency that fulfilled her in ways she did not expect. Later, she took a position as a bookkeeper for the Baptist church, a job that supported both her family and her faith. For such a deeply principled woman, it was a job match truly made in heaven.

It took me years to appreciate my mom's remarkable resiliency and her commitment to stay the course. She always got the job done, and never complained or blamed others for any hardship or problems life happened to hand her. Unfortunately, I never told her how much I respected these qualities until the end of her life, and then not directly.

During my last visit to her nursing home, I pushed her wheelchair into a quiet, sunny corner of a common room. The sun flooding through the floor-to-ceiling window was warm and it cut the chill of the day. I pulled a chair over and we sat silently enjoying the moment until she suddenly drew herself up as straight as possible in her wheelchair seat. She turned her head away from the light, smiled, and looked at me directly.

"Do you remember the family camping trips we always took when you and your brother were children?" she asked.

"I do," I replied, then added, "Those are some of the best memories of my life. I'm really glad to have them." She smiled and turned her face back to the sun.

"In fact," I said, realizing I was missing yet another opportunity to let her know just how much I appreciated her, "I'd say you and Dad did a fine job raising us. We've got nothing to complain about at all. You know that, don't you?"

She smiled and reached for my hand resting on her wheelchair's arm. She found a finger to wrap one of her own arthritic fingers around.

"I am so happy to hear you say that," she said giving my finger a good a strong squeeze. "We did the best we could, no matter what happened to us along the way. I guess it's all we expect to do in this life. I'm happy with how it all turned out." Then she released my finger and turned back to the sun. She seemed at peace, so I just let the moment of reconciliation speak for itself.

Grace and the Serenity Prayer

*Jeff Jackson and Suzanne Crichton on
their mother, Grace Jackson*

"God, grant me the serenity to accept the things I cannot change, courage to change the things I can, and wisdom to know the difference."

A visitor walking into our Brooklyn apartment might think that our family comprised recovering alcoholics or very religious Christians. The Serenity Prayer was always within view. Our mother, Grace, had it on paintings, decorative wall art, and tchotchkes strategically placed throughout our apartment. She had even hand-sewn them into a wall tapestry that greeted every visitor at the door.

Mom fervently believed in her ability to summon the courage to change the things she could. It was this belief that drove her values and her actions.

When my mom was pregnant with my sister, Suzanne, she was diagnosed with systemic lupus—a chronic autoimmune disease that would affect every aspect of her life. She spent most of the years after Suzanne was born in and out of hospitals. Her doctors gave her a list of "can't dos"—they told her she would never have another child, never live past 30, and never have a life that she would consider normal. She may have listened, but she never embraced their words.

Periodically, Mom would have lupus attacks. After one debilitating attack (I was around 12 years old at the time) her balance, equilibrium, and joints were severely affected. Mom put her arms around Suzanne's and Grandma's shoulders, and together they carefully walked into the doctor's office. During this visit, the doctor told her the next step would be a wheelchair. Mom's response was, "As long as I can fight, my children will never see me in a wheelchair."

Why did our mother respond this way? Lupus affected her ability to drive, because she could not judge distance. She had to rely on my father to do many things and she hated being dependent. Living in the suburbs made it even harder because she could not easily walk into town.

My mom had a strong sense of self, as well as a very specific image of how she presented herself to the world. It was an ongoing joke that whenever she got a haircut, we could never be sure what color it would be when she returned from the beauty parlor. Even when lying in a hospital bed, she would make sure that her hair and nails were done. This was something she could control.

As a mother of two, she was the caregiver. Lupus had taken

away her ability to work and her dream of becoming a lawyer. She was a mom first and foremost. This was what got her up every day and she made her children her priority. My mom's fight for the ability to walk (and avoid a wheelchair) also meant fighting for her role as a caregiver. She did not want to be cared for. She wanted to be a role model for us, and saw this as one of the many fights that she had to battle as a result of this disease.

Some of the details of what happened next have been lost over time, but one very important part of the story remains etched in our memory. After the doctor's appointment, my mother swore to herself (and anyone who would listen) that she would dance at my bar mitzvah. No one who knew her doubted that she would do so. She had fought back from much worse odds in the past.

Of course, if you knew my mom you also knew that she would not only dance at my bar mitzvah but also do it in fashionable heels. In the weeks prior to the party, she had my sister take her to a fancy shoe store and buy a pair of teal-colored heels that perfectly matched her dress.

Our family and friends were all aware of the doctor's comments and Mom's history leading into the bar mitzvah. When she walked out onto the dance floor for the mother and son dance, there was not a dry eye in the reception hall. My mom lived the words of the Serenity Prayer—she changed the things she could. All of this while wearing teal high heels and dancing to the 1979 Sister Sledge classic, "We Are Family."

Oh, the Places You'll Go!

JoAnn Duffy on her mother,
Elizabeth (Betty) McShane

When I was 24, I was living at home with my family in Philadelphia, engaged to be married, employed full time, and working on my master's degree. Then three weeks before my wedding, my future husband learned he was being transferred to Denver, Colorado, by his employer. This was completely unexpected and disruptive, and it terrified me. It would be a significant departure from the path we had planned. The change would affect our families as well. The oldest of six, I would be leaving my family to move across the country; it was overwhelming for me, as well as for my parents and siblings. In Denver, I did not have a place to live, a job, or a plan for completing my graduate studies. But my parents encouraged me to go, despite their strong desire to tell me to stay.

Without much time to process or plan, emotions were running high and my ambivalence was creating additional stress. I needed to make wedding and life decisions quickly. A natural leader, my dad helped me with the tangible aspects of moving, encouraging me along the way.

My mom gave me the Dr. Seuss book *Oh, the Places You'll Go!* While the book's intended audience is four- to eight-year-old children, my mom used it to frame a change for me in a way that was inspiring. She also reminded me of examples of courage and strength I had already overcome in my life, and assured me that those had prepared me for what was yet to come. She helped me understand that embracing this change would make me stronger, help me learn new things, and open doors. My mom helped me step out of my comfort zone and chart a different path. Her confidence gave me the strength to be open to this new journey and realize my potential. She pointed out the opportunity to show my brothers and sisters how to be successful by taking chances.

The day after our honeymoon, we moved to Denver. We found somewhere to live, I found my dream job, and I received a master's degree in social work. My husband and I became parents and took on our next challenge, caring for premature twins. Our journey to Denver prepared us well for managing this new life change.

You Don't Know Strength Until You Know My Mom

Jamie Watson on her mother, Rose Bosso

When my mother was a young woman in her mid-20s, she fell in love with and married a widower with four children, ranging in age from 10 to 15. She had an "instant" family and was soon expecting her first child (me). Then, three months into her pregnancy, the unthinkable happened. Her new husband had a massive heart attack and died.

My mother was pregnant and alone with four children who had lost both of their parents. My father was 38 when he passed away, and he had no will and no plan for his four children. The state wanted to place them in foster care, but my mother said no—she would raise them as her own. It was tough on her, but as a kid I never really knew. She was my mom, balancing the demands of everyday life and five kids.

Then when I was two, we lost everything in a flood. But still my mom persisted. My grandparents helped her, and so did one of my father's best friends. As time went on, my mom found love again with my dad's friend, and they were married when I was three.

The older kids settled into their teens, resentful toward my mom, but I never really felt the impact of that stress. She shouldered it all and was my protector. Eventually, my four step-siblings went off to college, and my mom and dad (the only one I've ever known) had my baby sister. We became a family of four, had a house, and things were good.

The reason I am successful is because of the example my mother set. Even when things were tough, no one knew it—she just made things happen. I've found myself in many challenging and even downright hard situations in my life. I think I always made it through because the grit my mother demonstrated is the same grit I show when faced with a challenge. I don't sweat the small stuff; instead I focus on doing the best I can with the hand I've been dealt. In most cases, I succeed. And when I don't, I've learned a whole lot in the process.

Managing Disruption

Bob Sachs on his mother, Irma Sachs

My parents began dating and then married soon after World War II. Dad was 21 and Mom was 19. They had both grown up in very comfortable, upper-middle-class homes in New York City. My dad joined my grandfather's successful retail business. I was born four years after they married. We moved to a nice house in the suburbs when I was a year old. My sister was born. A few years later, Dad started to manage their New Haven store. We moved into a fancier house in Connecticut, and Dad drove a fancy convertible. We joined a country club.

Dad hated the work. He left the business and started two others, but neither was successful and money became very tight. Gone were the club and the fancy car. Our big house became a three-bedroom, two-bath garden apartment. When I started junior high, we moved to a smaller two-bedroom, one-bath in a high rise. Our situation was better than many others, but it was a major change for us.

My mom's goal was to minimize the disruption in our lives. She would not be deterred. The move to the high rise was not easy, but she made it work. She insisted we keep the baby grand piano from her childhood and that I learned to play. I still remember watching the piano being hoisted four stories through the window into our living room. Because we only had two bedrooms, Mom had a wall built between the dining room and living room. Voilá, a bedroom for me. I entered through the kitchen. Cool! I thought it was a great.

While small, these tangible actions maintained a sense of stability for us all. We did not feel like we were moving backward. Most important, Mom encouraged us and told us that if we worked hard we could achieve our dreams. We stayed in that apartment until I was a senior in college. I wasn't there often once college began, but I still have fond memories of those years.

Finding Common Ground

Shannon Guiney Breuer on her mother,
Patrice McAllister Guiney

My mother loves math and science; I only barely passed chemistry because my sister tutored me. Mom loves reading the Sunday *New York Times* front to back; I love sailing. She knows all about ancient pharaohs and kings; I study business leaders. She studies the facts, while I study the feelings. She was the eldest of eight, and I was one of the middle children in a family of six girls.

My first memory of getting in trouble was at the age of five, when I invited 13 new neighbors to my house for a birthday party that my mother didn't know about. How was a girl in a new neighborhood to make new friends and get presents?

I only needed three quarters for prize money for the games we were going to play and a birthday cake. Thankfully there was enough time and humor in my mother's spirit to pull off making the cake, but I quickly learned my luck wouldn't always rescue me.

Our differences in opinion about what was important in life continued to emerge—why couldn't I play instead of study, watch TV instead of read, go to parties on a school night? Why were education and religion so important? To this day we still disagree about the college I attended.

As the years passed, the differences between my mother and me became walls that separated us even further. They caused us to be critical of each other even when times were good—like on my wedding day. We couldn't agree on anything from the invitation to the flowers, food, or people to invite. Instead of being a joyous day, it was filled with frustration and questions. Was I making these decisions in defiance of her or because I truly thought they were the right ones?

Being married gave me the chance to step away from her and to struggle—lose a job, suffer from a car accident, and get a divorce. It was then that I realized I could either continue blaming her for our differences or try to chart a new course. I was 33 years old and something needed to change. I could only change my attitude, but I didn't know quite how to go about it. So, I tried something new and so did she. When the criticism began during a conversation, we agreed to stop talking and try again later. Sometimes it meant short talks or quick and unexpected hang-ups, but the rule of law prevailed. No criticism allowed. It took months to feel the language change, but our demanding, no negative talk rule helped us focus on all the common ground that we shared but hadn't felt in years.

Since then I have remarried and now have two sons. What I have found to be most important are family, religion, and education. And giving back. My mom and I figured out that making a change begins with ourselves, no one else, and the values and beliefs she has always held were there for the taking. I just needed to see them.

Let Maude
Kick 'Em

Gilbert "Chuck" Davis on his grandmother
Thelma Davis-Spurill

Let Maude kick 'em! I can't begin to explain how many times I heard this saying throughout my childhood. It comes directly from my maternal grandmother, with whom I spent much time. In any discussion that ultimately ended in a lesson learned, she would simply close with a confirming loud Southern drawl, "Let Maude kick 'em!"

For example, if I was being stubborn about a specific task (not wanting to do schoolwork or not completing chores), the adults would discuss this and then all I would hear from my grandmother was, "Let Maude kick 'em!" More serious conversations involving adults led to the same outcome. When the final guidance was given and they still didn't listen and were determined to do it their way, all you would hear from my grandmother was, "Let Maude kick 'em!"

For years, I wondered and sometimes asked aloud, who was Maude? It wasn't until I was older that I realized that, to my grandmother, Maude was synonymous with life: If you don't want to listen to my advice, OK, life will show you better than I can tell you. According to my grandmother, family lore in Waterview, Virginia, had it that Maude was a very stubborn family mule who went back generations. How that transformed from, "Let life teach them" into, "Let Maude kick 'em," I have no idea, and will probably never know.

What I do know is that there is nothing more comical and at the same time more definitive than hearing my grandmother cringe, shake her head, and say, "Let Maude kick 'em" when she couldn't get through to a family member who was struggling with life choices.

Today, even when I can't get through to my children, I hear my grandmother's voice and ultimately blurt out, "Let Maude kick 'em," and everyone bursts into laughter at the memory of Nanny, who started it all and said it best!

Acknowledgments

We thank the many people who contributed to this book and who encouraged and supported us throughout this writing journey. *Leadership Lessons for Any Occasion: Stories of Our Mothers* would not have been possible without the dozens of contributors who wrote the stories about their mothers that comprise the book's seven chapters. The listing of these contributors and their short bios can be found near the end of the book. We also want to recognize and express our gratitude to the many others who submitted their own mom stories that, unfortunately, could not be included in this book.

Our sponsor, editors, and several other key professionals at ATD Press were invaluable partners. Ann Parker believed in us and the concept of this book. She sponsored and championed the approval process of our book proposal within ATD Press. Kathryn Stafford served as our developmental editor and patiently guided us through the manuscript development process. The copyediting of our manuscript was completed smoothly and professionally by Melissa Jones, the managing editor of ATD Press. Eliza Blanchard identified several young professionals who contributed very thoughtful stories, and

Jaime Brown worked with each contributor to secure their formal agreement to use their stories in our book.

Joel Goodman, founder and director of the HUMOR Project, is a friend of many years who, on numerous occasions, provided ideas, support, and encouragement for this book. Richard and Dolly Flasck regularly asked about the project and cheered us on during our annual winter visits to California.

We were inspired by the enthusiastic encouragement to write this book by our family members. Many thanks to Ari and Shauna Betof, Allison and Keith Warner, Nila's sister and brother-in-law Ronni and Jim Ozello, and Ed's brothers, Bob, John, and David. To our granddaughters, Anya and Kayla Betof, anticipating the fun you will have and the lessons you can learn from reading these stories was a constant source of motivation for us.

To the mothers of those who contributed their stories to this book, we honor you and thank you for the life and leadership lessons you have taught and the legacy you have left your children throughout their lives.

Thank you all!
Ed and Nila Betof

Reader's Guide: Using Stories at Work

Here are some easy-to-use ways to frame and communicate your unique leadership points of view using mom stories, sayings, and other dialogue starters.

Use your own mom stories and some from this book.
Leadership Lessons for Any Occasion: Stories of Our Mothers has dozens of mom stories on teaching, coaching, supporting others, having vision and hope, courage, demonstrating resolve and humility, innovating while leading others, and managing change. Any one or several of these stories could be used to set the stage for you to discuss your unique leadership perspectives on those or other topics. Here are two examples we have used to communicate our unique leadership perspectives when we teach.

Supporting Others' Hopes and Dreams

When I was younger, I was a serious skater. I spent hours each morning before school practicing figures over and over on a small, rectangular piece of ice called a patch. Learning those figures is a disciplined process; it's not the fun jumps and spins that we all think of when we watch the Olympics. Skating on a patch is cold and it's lonely, demanding precision and stamina.

There were just a few of us up at such an early time, but if I was up early, my mother would be up even earlier. She would stand at the oven and cook breakfast for me, make sure I had all my skating equipment, and get me to the rink. My mother never complained about her loss of sleep; she never asked me to stop skating or to change my practice time to make her life easier.

My mother understood that this time alone on the ice concentrating as hard as I could and doing these small, intricate maneuvers over and over would help me build the skills I needed later in life. I may not have made it to the Olympics, but I learned important leadership lessons from those early mornings. I learned the value of supporting others' hopes and dreams, which is vital in my work as a business leader and executive coach. By supporting other peoples' aspirations, you earn their respect and trust, which greatly increases your positive influence with them.

—Nila Betof

The All-Star Game and the Bus to A.C.

When I was 14 years old, baseball was a very important part of my life. I worked hard at school and had several part-time jobs, and girls had entered my adolescent world. But baseball was my thing.

One day in late June, I was notified that I was one of two players on our team to be selected for a citywide, all-star team. This was a highlight in my life at the time, and I was very proud to be selected.

When I shared my good news with my mom and

dad, they were very happy for me. But when we looked at the calendar (the dreaded calendar), I was dismayed to see that the game was scheduled during our annual family vacation in Atlantic City, New Jersey. This week-long vacation was a family highlight for my parents as well as my three brothers and me. Now we, or was it I, had a dilemma. From my parents' perspective, there was no question, I would have to miss the citywide all-star game. Our family vacation took precedence. I was heartbroken.

My mom was always empathetic and highly sensitive to the needs of others. The term had not yet been invented, but my mother had a remarkably high level of emotional intelligence. When, after several days, my disappointment had not waned, she decided to come up with a solution. She convinced my dad that I was old enough and responsible enough to stay home, by myself, for two days so I could play in the all-star game. Then I could take the bus from downtown Philadelphia to A.C. to join my family for the rest of the vacation. This decision had everything to do with trust and respect for something I had worked very hard to achieve and wanted to participate in very badly.

Six weeks later, my family left for A.C. in our old 1955 Chevrolet station wagon. I stayed behind and played shortstop in the all-star game the following day. Early the next morning, I boarded the bus for Atlantic City.

This event was more than a simple chapter in the life of a 14-year-old kid. It was a building block for one of my most important life and leadership lessons. I learned the vital importance of earning trust and creating the conditions for strengthening trust with others. Throughout my leadership career, I have gone out of my way early and often to create the conditions for team members, colleagues, and other key stakeholders to feel as though they can trust me. In turn, this makes it easier than it might otherwise be for trust to flow back and forth. Trust speeds up almost everything and, for this, I have been rewarded many times over.

—Ed Betof

Use one of your own stories to help others start to keep their own active story files.

Select your own sayings or expressions, such as the following, as a lead-in or to integrate into your story.

Nila's mother used to say, "You can't put your head on their shoulders." She has used this to help leaders understand that they can't always transfer their knowledge and experience by simply telling others what they know. Sometimes people need to learn lessons on their own and live with the consequences of their choices.

Ed's mother often said, "Time has a wonderful way of finding solutions that are not evident today." He often uses this expression to counter his own impatience.

Be inspired by important life events to generate stories.

For example, we all have successes and failures in our lives and careers. Did your mother help you deal with these periods? How so? During significant, possibly life-changing events or turning points, how did your mother or others support you?

Describe your beliefs.

Did your mother teach you any life or leadership lessons related to any of the following topics? Consider how you could bring these lessons into your story or discussion of your unique leadership perspective:

- business growth, purpose, vision, and legacy
- teamwork and trust
- disciplined execution
- talent management and leadership development
- decision making and judgment calls
- courage, resilience, and grit
- resourcefulness and innovation
- drive and work ethic
- integrating fierce resolve and personal humility
- relationships.

Be interviewed or interview others.

Use questions to generate stories of a person's unique leadership perspective. For each, how did your mother influence you? Consider integrating that mom story or anecdote into your comments. Here are some starting points for your interview:

- What do you value most?
- What do you deeply believe?
- What were moments of truth in your life and what did you learn from them?
- What were the turning points in your life?
- What do you want your legacy to be?
- What is your leadership platform?
- What was the best advice or feedback you ever received? From whom did you receive it? How did you use it?

Use visual images and narratives to present or discuss your unique leadership perspective.

We like to use images to generate or share stories that represent our unique leadership perspectives. Perhaps you want to include pictures of your mom or family. Or if you don't want to do that, you can also find free and paid images of every imaginable topic on sites such as iStock or Unsplash. The Center for Creative Leadership's Visual Explorer has more than 200 highly memorable images available for use.

Use famous or meaningful quotes to help describe and discuss your unique leadership perspective.

Ask others to contribute and describe their quotes and the story behind the quotes. For example, Bill Kozy, former chief operating officer at BD, was influenced deeply in his career by a quote from his mother, Lanila Kozy:

> "I do not care what you decide to do in your work—just decide that you will be the best at it. When you do a job—big or small—do it right . . . or not at all."

Anyone who knows or has ever worked with Bill knows that he lives and has worked in a way that is 100 percent consistent with that message. Here are few of our favorite quotes:

- "Yesterday is history, tomorrow is a mystery, today is a gift. That is why they call it the present." —Eleanor Roosevelt
- "Thinking is hard. That is why most people judge." — Carl Jung
- "People don't care how much you know until they know how much you care." —Dick Vermeil
- "Good is the enemy of great." —Jim Collins
- "Luck favors the prepared mind." —Louis Pasteur
- "Little things affect little minds." —Benjamin Disraeli
- "The conductor doesn't make a sound. The power of the conductor is derived from making other people feel powerful." —Ben Zander, Conductor for the Boston Philharmonic

About the Contributors

Donna M. Beestman | President and Executive Career Strategist, Career Success Strategies

For more than 25 years Donna has served as a career transition strategist and executive coach, holding leadership roles with regional and international career management consulting firms. She was also a performance manager for a firm serving Fortune 500 firms, executive director of an education policy nonprofit, and a high school faculty member. Donna has served on many boards related to public policy, women in leadership, university alumni, regional theater, and Rotary.

John Betof | Retired Teacher

John taught industrial arts, computers, and career prep to junior high students for 30 years in New Jersey and Arizona. He and wife, Sharyn, have one son and two grandchildren. Now retired, John lives in Utah, where he enjoys cycling, hiking, snowshoeing, gardening, and being a grandpa.

Robert J. Betof | Artist and Illustrator

Robert studied at the Pennsylvania Academy of the Fine Arts, University of Pennsylvania, Temple University, and the Barnes Foundation, as well as independent study in Europe. He has won many awards for his work and has had numerous exhibitions. Robert also worked as a teacher and administrator. He is now semi-retired to his studio, is an avid gardener, and teaches kayaking.

Shauna Wilson Betof | Program and Sponsorship Manager, AISNE
In addition to her work at AISNE, Shauna is the co-chair of the National Association of Independent Schools Families First program, which supports heads of schools and their families across the country. She's also on the board of directors for the Brookline Education Foundation. Prior to that, she was an assistant athletic director at George School and was awarded a Lang Grant to examine connections between physical activity, learning, and brain development. After playing soccer at Cornell University, Shauna was an Olympic development soccer coach, a graduate assistant for the women's soccer team at Springfield College, and the director of a soccer club.

Mark Bocianski | Vice President, Global Head of Talent Management and Learning, Western Union Company
Prior to joining HP, Mark was the global head of talent development at Aon Hewitt, a leading provider of human resources consulting and outsourcing services. While there, he was focused on driving all learning, performance, succession management, leadership development, and employee engagement. Over his 17-year tenure with the company, Mark held numerous roles including the implementation of HR outsourcing solutions, managing outsourcing operations, and leading a business unit. Mark holds a bachelor of arts in education from Northeastern Illinois University. He resides in Dana Point, California.

Donna Boles | President and Founder, Sisters Enlisted to Empower Dreams
Donna served as senior vice president of human resources at Becton, Dickinson and Company until her retirement in 2013 after a 40-year career. She now serves as an advisory board member for Cielo Healthcare and is on the board of trustees for the Berkeley College Foundation. Donna also served on the board for CST Brands as the compensation committee chair, and served as board chair for Big Brothers Big Sisters of Northern New Jersey. In 2016, she became a National Association of Corporate Directors Board Leadership Fellow.

Shannon Guiney Breuer | President and Chief Compliance Officer, Wiley Group

Shannon spent the majority of her career in human relations and communications leadership roles at Sunoco Inc. *SmartCEO* magazine recognized Shannon with a 2016 BRAVA Award and *Philadelphia Business Journal* named her a Women of Distinction in 2010. She is an executive board member of the Forum of Executive Women, and is active with many nonprofit and professional groups, speaking on career transition, corporate culture, and business networking. A graduate of Marymount University, Shannon and her husband have two grown sons.

Chuck Burak | Former Director, Worldwide Benefits, BD

Chuck's professional career spanned 35 years in the HR total rewards arena, with the last 21 at BD, a global medical technology company. Before joining BD in 1990, he worked for a diverse range of organizations, including Met Life, ITT Corporation, and KPMG. His many areas of focus included HR transformation, budget management, vendor management, global retirement plan design and administration, mergers and acquisitions, and wealth management counseling. He graduated from Queens College with a bachelor of arts in mathematics.

Chris Cappy | Founder and President, Pilot Consulting Corporation

Chris has worked as a keynote speaker, consultant, and executive coach in more than 40 countries as an expert in change management, executive development, and experiential change leadership education. He is the author of *Driving Leaders: Lessons in High-Performance Leadership Drawn From Endurance Racing.* He lives in Colorado with his wife, Andrea, and his son, Allen Joseph.

Douglas N. Clayton | Senior Vice President, Talent Management and Learning and Development, SES

Doug splits his time between SES's Princeton location and the Luxembourg headquarters. He is also a documentary filmmaker and has produced several parodies of mainstream movies, including James Bond films, *The Godfather, Star Trek,* and *Mission Impossible.* Doug earned a doctorate degree from the University of Pennsylvania, and is an alumnus of the Wharton Business School. He conducts ongoing research, has been published, and is a speaker on the topic of film and learning.

Suzanne Crichton | Mother and Grandmother

Suzanne was the primary caregiver for her twins, who are now in their mid-20s. As a stay-at-home mom and grandmother, she has weathered all storms, managed all types of chaos, and helped her kids and grandkids find their way in the world.

Alicia E. Daughtery | Vice President, Customer Experience, Comcast Cable

Alicia helps to execute transformational initiatives on behalf of Comcast's customers and employees. She holds a bachelor of electrical engineering from the University of Delaware and an MBA from Villanova. A graduate of the Comcast Women in Leadership Program at Wharton and the Betsy Magness Leadership Institute, Alicia serves as a mentor to young women and was recognized with the Connect Award from Women in Cable Telecommunications. The proud parents of two grown children, Jay and Leah, Alicia and her husband, Jim, are award-winning home brewers and reside in Pennsylvania.

Gilbert (Chuck) Davis | Assistant Vice President, Associate Chief Information Officer, Children's Hospital of Philadelphia

Prior to joining Children's Hospital of Philadelphia (CHOP) in 2007, Gilbert worked in a variety of healthcare leadership roles. He has more than 28 years of experience in various aspects of healthcare administration and IT. Gilbert currently serves on multiple advisory boards, including in an advisory capacity to the CEO of CHOP as a member of the Diversity and Inclusion Advisory Council. He also serves as a fiduciary board director for a nonprofit that prepares children for college and careers in science, technology, engineering, and math.

Peter J. Dean | Founder and President, Leaders By Design

Peter founded Leaders by Design in 1986 and has coached executives in more than 50 companies, including those in Europe and Asia. He has also taught courses in leadership and communication at the Wharton School at the University of Pennsylvania, Penn State University, Fordham University, the University of Iowa, and the University of Tennessee. While at the University of Tennessee, he co-designed their online physician Executive MBA program. He received teaching awards at Penn State, the Wharton School, and the University of Tennessee. Peter has authored 10 books and numerous articles, and was also the editor for *Performance Improvement Quarterly* for six years.

Lynne DeLay | Managing Partner, One World Leaders

With a doctorate in management and a diploma in coaching supervision from Coaching Supervision Academy (UK), Lynne's career as a leadership coach, mentor, and coach supervisor spans more than 25 years and three continents. She has coached senior executives from across the globe, and, as an accredited coach supervisor, has provided supervision to coaches from multiple countries to help them stay on the leading edge of their work. Lynne was previously the director of coaching with the Center for Creative Leadership in Europe, where she lived for 25 years.

Rick DeSouza | Associate Broker, Re/Max Eastern

After Rick graduated from Penn State in 1975, his dad suggested he get a real estate license in case things didn't work out. So, he did. Rick eventually founded the DeSouza Realty Group. He and his wife, Andi, joined Re/Max Eastern in 2016, which brought them full circle back to Philadelphia. They have two children, Spencer and Morgan.

Dave Drabot | Former Manager, Towers Perrin

Dave worked for four large organizations principally in the area of enterprise-wide application systems development and management. He graduated from Penn State University in 1975 with an MPA and a focus on information systems technology.

JoAnn Duffy | Social Work Operations Manager, Children's Hospital of Philadelphia

JoAnn is responsible for the operations and administrative oversight of the division of social work at Children's Hospital of Philadelphia, which includes more than 160 social workers. She previously worked in informal and formal leadership roles in older adult protective services and several health systems, including University of Colorado and Temple University. She is also a board officer on the board of directors for Make-A-Wish Philadelphia, Delaware, and Susquehanna Valley.

Marion Molineaux Feigenbaum | Senior Vice President of Conferences, The Conference Board

Marion started her career at the Conference Board as a research assistant on Manufacturers' Capital Appropriations after graduating from Barnard College with a degree in economics. Happily, she escaped economics and loves working on creating more than 75 conferences annually.

Jennifer Finkelstein | Certified Employees Assistance Professional, Federal Occupational Health

Jennifer has worked for Federal Occupational Health for more than 15 years. In her role, she provides counseling to a wide range of employees with various psychological issues. She is also in charge of writing and presenting on various wellness topics. Jennifer also provided crisis intervention services after national disasters, including Hurricanes Harvey, Irene, and Maria. She has twin boys.

Dodi Fordham | Senior Sales Consultant, Carlisle Collection

Over the past 28 years, Dodi has had the privilege of working with wonderful women to help make them look and feel their very best by developing infinitely useful wardrobes. Styles and fashions change, but the need for a woman to present herself in exactly the right way never changes. Dodi looks forward to continuing to assist in the process of making her clients appear as fabulous as they feel.

John Gillis Jr. | President, LeadershipX

John facilitates executive leadership development programs for cross-industry companies around the globe using a digital business simulation based on his doctoral dissertation. Previously, he worked for IBM's Strategic Change consulting, Accenture, and the Center for Creative Leadership. John has also served as president of the Penn Doctoral Alumni Network, on boards for Young Life and the Austin Leadership Forum, as a Scout Cub Master, and as coach of numerous sports teams. He is also the founder of CampLIFE!, a nonprofit charity with a mission to provide for the families of deceased soldiers.

Jay Glasscock | Chief Transformation Officer, Owens & Minor

Jay is an executive with more than 20 years of diversified leadership experience in the medical device and life science industry. Prior to joining Owens & Minor, he was the vice president and general manager, clinical diagnostics, at Thermo Fisher Scientific. He also enjoyed a successful career with Becton, Dickinson, where he held several key roles. Jay is passionate about business leadership, teaching leadership development, and strategy execution. He enjoys hiking, skiing, and riding his horses.

Neal R. Goodman | President and CEO, Global Dynamics Inc.

Neal is an internationally recognized authority on cultural competence, inclusion, and organization development. His training programs have helped more than a million corporate leaders succeed in global and diverse environments. Neal is a professor emeritus at Saint Peter's University. He is also a columnist and keynote speaker who is often quoted in leading publications. He is married with two daughters and three grandchildren (so far).

Jane Barr Horstman | CEO, Jane Barr Horstman & Associates (JBHA)

After founding her company more than 30 years ago, Jane now employs 10 women who handle the day-to-day working of the business. JBHA specializes in three areas: association management, special event coordination, and personal assistants in wealthy homes. She resides with her husband, John, in Fort Washington, Pennsylvania.

June Howard | Senior Vice President and Chief Accounting Officer, Aflac Incorporated

June joined Aflac in 2009 and was named chief accounting officer a year later. Before joining Aflac, she held financial reporting positions of continuing responsibility at ING and The Hartford. Additionally, she worked as an auditor with Ernst & Young for nearly 10 years. June graduated from the University of Alabama in Huntsville with a bachelor's degree in business administration. She is married and has two children, John and Mary. Her hobbies include running, reading, scrapbooking, and playing piano.

Jerry Hurwitz | Retired Executive Vice President and Chief Human Resource Officer, BD

Jerry was a member of BD's senior management team, serving in HR and business roles over his 25-year career. His focus was on developing leaders at all levels of the organization. He is an executive fellow with the Center for Higher Ambition Leadership, an organization dedicated to developing purpose-driven leaders and organizations. Jerry is also a member of the UNC Wilmington Cameron School of Business

Executive Network and the Wilmington Investors Network, an angel group focused on investing in early stage start-up companies. He lives in Wilmington, North Carolina, where he finds time for kayaking, traveling, and playing pickleball.

Jeff Jackson | Leadership Consultant, Experience to Lead

Jeff is the proud father of two teenagers. In his spare time, he is also the program director for experiential programs with the Conference Board and the co-founder of Experience to Lead, where he's responsible for business development and client relationships. Jeff previously worked as the executive director of leadership and experiential programs for the Conference Board. In that capacity he was responsible for the delivery of more than 100 customized executive and C-level leadership and best practice programs.

Ted Kauffman | President, Kauffman Holdings

Ted is the bio-founder and chairman of Eastern Connection Operating. Founded in 1983, Eastern Connection is a logistics company with 17 facilities scattered throughout the northeastern part of the United States. After a few years, Eastern Connection expanded into the messenger business and then into the outsourcing space a few years after that. After selling Eastern Connection, Ted founded Kauffman Holdings in 2015. This company invests in alternative strategies and purchases and builds small companies. Ted lives in New York with his 19-year-old son.

Sabrina Kay | Entrepreneur and Philanthropist

Sabrina is a serial entrepreneur and philanthropist who started seven diverse ventures, including Art Institute of Hollywood and Premier Business Bank. She is most passionate about her current role as chancellor and CEO of Fremont College. Her awards include Woman of the Year by the California Legislature, Finalist for Entrepreneur of the Year by Ernst & Young, and induction into the Hall of Fame by the California Association of Postsecondary Schools. Sabrina holds a doctorate degree in work-based learning leadership from the University of Pennsylvania and double master's degrees from USC and GSE at the University of Pennsylvania.

Renée Owens Kennish | Former Vice President, ValueOptions Federal Services

Renée has more than 30 years of experience in various leadership roles, primarily in the behavioral health arena. In her most recent position, she provided executive oversight for all operational and administrative components of a large $500 million federal program, providing behavioral health and work-life services, including overall quality, productivity, efficiency, and organizational readiness of call centers across the United States. Renée currently consults on various projects, including management consultation and project support for strategic planning, call center operations, quality and productivity, design and development of proposal strategies, and marketing and strategic communications.

William A. Kozy | Former Executive Vice President and Chief Operating Officer, BD

William was a member of the senior management team at BD and served in various executive vice president roles. He is currently a member of the Cooper Companies board of directors and sits on the audit committee and science and technology committee. He is also a member of Hackensack Meridian Health Board of Governors, and serves on the strategic planning committee, the executive and physician compensation committee, and health ventures board. William resides in Naples, Florida, with his wife, Carol, and frequently hosts their family.

Jean Larkin | Talent Management and Leadership Development Executive

Jean is the former vice president of talent development at Johnson Controls, and is now consulting with individuals and organizations on talent strategy and career development. She is a global human resources executive and talent strategist with exceptional accomplishment in designing and implementing unique and meaningful talent solutions, C-suite and board-level advisement, and sustainable talent systems in consumer, insurance, industrial, and technology companies experiencing or requiring significant transformations. She holds a doctorate in education from the University of Pennsylvania and is a volunteer career coach for military veterans.

Bob Levin | Features Editor, the *Globe and Mail*

Bob Levin is an award-winning journalist who is currently a features editor at the *Globe and Mail* in Toronto. A graduate of the Columbia School of Journalism, he spent five years as a *Newsweek* writer in New York before moving on to *Maclean's,* where over two decades he served as a writer, columnist, and executive editor. Bob also writes fiction; his novel *Away Game* was published in 2016.

Jennifer Hanson Long | Instructional Designer, Learning and Development, Schwan's Company

Jennifer's coolest "fun fact" is that she is a triplet. And no, they are not identical (she has two brothers), and yes, her mom dressed them alike. She currently works at Schwan's Company in Minnesota as an instructional designer in learning and development. Jennifer received a master's degree from North Dakota State University and a bachelor's degree from Concordia College. She is an aspiring writer and speaker and loves sharing stories from her sitcom of a life.

Alejandra Love | National Director, Professional Development, Phalen Leadership Academies

In her tenure at Phalen Leadership Academies, Alejandra created and launched a blended learning professional development model, including building from the ground up the highly immersive online learning program called PLA University. Alejandra manages the professional development of more than 300 educators, ultimately serving more than 4,000 students throughout the Midwest each year. Alejandra is passionate about professional development and youth; in her free time, she volunteers as a college and career coach for high school seniors, and plays with her beautiful daughter, Kennedy Amiyah.

Maqsood Mamawala | Executive Coach

As an executive coach, Maqsood's forte is leadership development programs for managers and executives. He's driven to help clients reach their own "next phase" by partnering with them to find ways to quickly improve skills and competencies to achieve their goals, be they professional, personal, or both. Whether assisting individual contributors, a team of associates, or managers, Maqsood's committed to helping them find ways to enhance their practice, team, or company. His coaching work reaches a variety of industries and disciplines, including marketing and sales businesses, engineering, operations, financial services, government, manufacturing, and nonprofits.

Lisa Mathis | Principal, Parker Consulting

Lisa brings an incredible amount of hands-on experience in executive coaching, leadership, communications, and organization development. She has expertise in working with high potentials to the COO level, as well as understanding different cultures and the challenges that they face. She prepares leaders for the next level by building new competencies, imparting advice on leading change, and enhancing decision-making skills. She works with specific targets and measures that are reflected in the development action plan that the executives create under her guidance and coaching.

Mary McDowell | Former Senior Legislative Staff, Alaska State Legislature

Mary's professional career, in both state government and the private sector, focused primarily on Alaskan fisheries. Besides hands-on work in commercial fishing and fish buying, she served as a senior legislative aide, specializing in fisheries and other natural resource issues; a special assistant for fisheries and wildlife to the governor of Alaska; commissioner of the Commercial Fisheries Entry Commission; and vice president of Pacific Seafood Processors Association.

Susannah McMonagle | Assistant Professor, Communication Studies, Eastern University

Susannah teaches in the communication studies department at Eastern University. Her research interests include global advertising, global communication, social media, and public relations. Before earning a PhD from Temple University in media and communication, Susannah worked in corporate communication for nearly seven years with leadership development firm the Leader's Edge/Leaders By Design. She resides in Phoenixville, Pennsylvania, with her husband and daughter.

Donna McNamara | Former Vice President, Global Education and Training, Colgate Palmolive

Donna developed Colgate's world-wide learning strategy, designed its business goal alignment process, and built leadership capability in accelerating effective change. She is past board chair of ATD, a recipient of the Gordon M. Bliss Award for distinguished contribution, and a former member of ATD's Board of Directors. Donna is currently a trustee at St. Catherine University and the College of St. Elizabeth. Additionally, she is a board member for the distinctive women's philanthropic organization, Impact 100 Garden State.

Winni McNamara | Advanced Nurse Practitioner

Shortly after completing a BS in 1973, Winni heard the word *midwife* and knew that was her path. She has worked as a private practice advanced registered nurse practitioner, specializing in women's health and midwifery, since 1980 and has delivered more than 3,000 babies. She is also a graduate of the Hahnemann College of Homeopathy. Winni lives in the Pacific Northwest with her husband of 41 years. In her private time she enjoys hiking and gardening.

Chad Merritt | Vice President, Americas Sales,
Center for Creative Leadership

For the last 15 years, Chad has served in sales roles for the Center for Creative Leadership, a global nonprofit focused on leadership development and recognized as an elite executive education provider. Chad worked with companies of all sizes, including nonprofits, NGOs, and education providers, focusing on facilitating discussions about how their leaders can have more impact on the lives they touch every day in their companies, in their communities, and at home.

Mike Mersky | Head, Saint Edward's School

Mike, a product of Friends' Central School in Philadelphia, has taught, coached, and led independent schools throughout his 42-year career. His wife, Karen, is a licensed clinical psychologist with a PhD from Bryn Mawr College. His son, Matt, a graduate of Lafayette College and Duke's Fuqua School of Business, is a consultant for PwC. His daughter Kathryn, a graduate of Dickinson College and University of Pennsylvania, is the dean of student affairs at Springside Chestnut Hill Academy in Philadelphia. Karen and Mike reside in Vero Beach, Florida.

Mark Morrow | Writer and Book Development Consultant

Mark is a freelance book developer and writer specializing in management, leadership, workplace learning, organization development, and human resources. Previously he was manager of acquisition and development for ASTD Press (now ATD Press), as well as an executive editor for McGraw-Hill's professional book division. As a journalist, Mark wrote for a variety of newspapers, trade and professional newsletters, and magazines; he has also worked on assignments for *People, Esquire, Fortune,* and other national and regional magazines and newspapers as a freelance photographer.

Eunice Sevilla Nuyles | Senior Director, Global Customer Ops & Support, LexisNexis Risk Solutions

Armed with 13 years of success leading customer support teams for organizations across multiple disciplines, Eunice moved to Atlanta from Manila in 2015 to lead B2B support operations in a risk management technology industry. She is a visionary customer experience leader, enabling customer service professionals to embrace their role in driving customer loyalty. She works actively as the co-chair for the Lean-In Circle committee under LexisNexis Risk Solutions Women Connected Group, where she interacts with women leaders and professionals, advocating strongly for their development and career advancement. She enjoys traveling with her husband, Niko, and their sons, Nicholas and Ethan.

James Pasquale Orlando | Associate Chief Academic Officer, St. Luke's University Health Network

James serves as associate chief academic officer at St. Luke's University Health Network in Bethlehem, Pennsylvania. He also serves as course director and lecturer at University of Pennsylvania's Graduate School of Education, and as an adjunct professor at Moravian College's MBA program. James is a clinical associate professor in the department of psychiatry at Sidney Kimmel Medical College. He earned an EdD from University of Pennsylvania in 2009 and was named one of *Training* magazine's 2011 Top 10 Young Trainers. He served in the U.S. Army Reserves for 10 years and lives with his wife, Missy, and three children in Macungie, Pennsylvania.

Lisa MD Owens | Founder, Training Design Strategies

After a 30-year career at Procter & Gamble in engineering and global learning, Lisa retired and founded Training Design Strategies to continue doing what she does best: Working with the world's doers and movers to help them achieve their goals with the help of powerful training. She earned a BCHe from Georgia Tech in 1977 and an MEd from the University of Cincinnati in 1996. She is an author, speaker, and trainer, and is learning how to quit. She and her husband of 40 years have two children and a grandchild.

James C. Ozello | Founder and President, Human Resources Services
Jim is a pioneer in the outsourcing of HR services to small and growing companies that do not have in-house professional human resource management. Prior to establishing his firm in 1975, Jim gained experience in HR management, sales, marketing, accounting, finance, and manufacturing with Shell Oil Company, AT&T, Mattel, and Carter Hawley Hale. He is instrumental in advancing HR services that reflect the culture and vision of the companies he serves. Jim presently serves as executive vice president, human resources, for Kennedy Wilson Holdings. An author and lecturer, Jim conducts seminars and workshops for industry groups and client companies.

Ronni Goodman Ozello | Former Assistant Vice Principal, Special Education
Ronni received a bachelor of science degree in elementary education from Temple University and then taught in the Philadelphia Public School System. Upon moving to Los Angeles, she then taught in the Los Angeles Unified School System. Ronni then earned a master's degree in educational administration and was promoted to assistant principal. She collaborated with parents, teachers, psychologists, physical and occupational therapists, and speech therapists to create individualized programs for students with special needs. After retiring from her full-time position, Ronni continued as an intervention teacher tutoring students in reading and mathematics.

Howard Prager | President, Advance Learning Group
Howard Prager has significant experience in leadership and talent development. He is president of Advance Learning Group, a learning and leadership consulting firm, as well as the creator of Make Someone's Day, a movement to increase appreciation for one another. Howard is a volunteer leader in the Boy Scouts of America, North-

western Alumni Association, and ATD. He also plays tuba with the Northwest Concert Band, the Royal Blue Tinkertoy Dixieland Band, and other groups. His mother is his most dedicated groupie, traveling as far as Germany and Italy with his bands.

Sharon Collins Presnell | Chief Scientific Officer, Organovo, and President, Samsara Sciences

Sharon completed her undergraduate education at North Carolina State University and received a PhD in experimental pathology from the Medical College of Virginia. After postdoctoral training and a junior faculty position at the University of North Carolina at Chapel Hill, she transitioned to industry and has held multiple R&D and business leadership roles at Becton Dickinson, Tengion, Organovo, and Samsara Sciences. Sharon dedicates her free time to mentoring, writing, and spending time with family. She serves on the board of the College of Life Sciences Foundation at North Carolina State University.

Maribeth D. Renne | Career and Leadership Coach

Maribeth is a seasoned career and leadership coach whose mission is to empower people with the knowledge, tools, and skills to be success- ful, effective, and fulfilled in their work. She coaches individuals to become thoughtful and powerful leaders and deliver results for their organizations. Her clients come from leading corporations, nonprof- its, and higher education institutions all over the United States. In addition to her clients, she shares the lessons she learned from her mother with her children, Christopher and Elizabeth.

Teresa Roche | Chief Human Resources Officer, City of Fort Collins

Believing that creating and sustaining healthy, inclusive, and econom- ically viable communities can change the world, Teresa is living a path of purpose in her current position. She has worked as an executive in a variety of high-technology companies, helping them through various stages of their organizational life cycles, including startups, acquisi- tions, mergers, splits, and divestitures. Teresa is a fellow with Harvard University's Learning and Innovation Laboratory and has a PhD in education from Purdue University. She is married to David Monahan, and their daughter, Kai Monahan, is attending the University of Denver, studying theater, creative writing, and gender and women's studies.

Sharon Dobin Ross | Former Human Resources Information Systems Manager

Upon graduating as an education major from Temple University, Sharon was an elementary school teacher for the Philadelphia Public School System. After raising four children, she was in human resource systems as HRIS manager for more than 24 years at The PQ Corporation until retirement.

Bob Sachs | Advisory Chair, The Leadership Development Group

Bob's book on leading across the health ecosystem, co-written with The Leadership Development Group's CEO, will be published this fall. He also sits on the board of We Care Services for Children, which provides mental health and developmental services to children in the San Francisco Bay area. Bob was vice president, national learning and development, for 19 years at Kaiser Permanente. While there, his responsibilities included leadership development, succession management, and learning. Prior to that, Bob was a general manager and partner at the Hay Group, a global consultancy.

Sara Beth Schneider | Onboarding Specialist, Samaritan's Purse

Sara Beth grew up in Birmingham, Alabama, where she and her two younger brothers were raised on sweet tea, humidity, and "Roll Tide!" After attending Furman University, Sara Beth joined Samaritan's Purse, an international relief organization based in North Carolina. It was there in North Carolina that she met her husband, Coty. They happily reside in the small mountain town of Boone, along with their adorable goldendoodle, Moses.

David Smith | HR Generalist for the Town of Smyrna, TN

David thoroughly enjoys his work as an HR generalist in local government simply because he gets to help others. Through his work in training, advising, counseling, and encouraging, he is able to remain connected to what matters most in any organization: the people. David received a bachelor's degree in mass communication from the University of Southern Mississippi and is currently seeking a master's in HR management.

Molly D. Shepard | CEO and President, The Leader's Edge/Leaders By Design

Molly founded The Leader's Edge in 2001 to address the leadership development of senior women in business. She has more than 30 years' experience in leadership development and executive coaching, and has served on for-profit and not-for-profit boards. Recognized for her leadership in the Philadelphia community, Molly often speaks as a thought leader in women's leadership development. She has written four books including *The Bully-Proof Workplace* (written with Peter Dean, 2017) and *Breaking Into the Boys' Club* (2015).

Alanna Steffen-Nelson | Clinical Project Manager, Cook Research Incorporated

Prior to working at Cook Research, Alanna was a lab manager and postdoctoral research associate at Howard Hughes Medical Institute. She was a doctoral student in biological sciences at Purdue University, and an instructor and teaching assistant at Earlham College.

Lew Stern | Former President, Stern Consulting

Lew Stern has consulted for and coached leaders on five continents for more than 40 years. He has taught at the graduate level for several universities and has conducted research and published on psychological applications in organizations, especially on leadership development. He now donates his time to nonprofits and initiatives focused on environmental sustainability, peaceful resolution of differences, and quality of life. His mother and father, Marilyn and Saul Stern, have served as role models of compassion and giving.

David Turner | Former Teacher and Owner, The Closet Doctor

David started his career as a high school math teacher, baseball coach, and gymnastics coach at Cherry Hill High School. When he left teaching, David and his wife, Joyce, started the Closet Doctor, a business providing custom closet design and installations in new and existing homes. He was president and CFO, while Joyce served as vice president and managed sales and client accounts. They retired in Venice, Florida, but visit frequently with their two married children and four grandchildren in Medford, New Jersey, and New York City.

Jamie Watson | Procurement Manager, Toyota Financial Services

As procurement manager, Jamie is responsible for supplier registration, enterprise vendor management, supplier diversity, third-party spend reporting, and enterprise process automation at Toyota Financial Services (TFS). She has been at TFS more than nine years, holding various management positions throughout her career. Jamie is the co-chair of TFS's Team IMPACT (Integrating Meaningful Partnerships Across Community and Toyota) and engages team members across the company to volunteer in the community. She is also a sponsor of the TFS Diverse & Small Business Supplier Mentorship Program. Jamie, her husband, Byron, and their son, Jayden, live in The Colony, Texas.

Craig Weakley | Vice President, Western Region, 20th Television

With more than 25 years of experience in the media and entertainment industry, Craig has sold the syndication rights to more than 60 different television shows, ranging from *M.A.S.H.* to *The Simpsons.* He is currently vice president, Western region, for 20th Television, the domestic syndication division of 20th Century Fox. Craig graduated from UCLA in 1989 with a BA in history. He is an avid golfer, loves to travel, and enjoys spending time with his daughters, Alyssa and Alexis.

Wendy York Witterschein | Former Director, Global Learning, BD University, BD

Wendy is a talent development, learning, and business leader, with experience in a variety of learning and business development activities. Her career spans multibillion-dollar global corporations and senior-level consulting with Fortune 500 companies. Wendy is an expert in the areas of organization development, executive coaching, and team acceleration. She holds two master's degrees, and is a PhD candidate in psychology and education with focus on thinking and reasoning at Columbia University. Wendy does original research in mental models, a key component of business transformation and cultural change for individuals, teams, and organizations.

About the Authors

 **Ed Betof, EdD,** is a leader, teacher, coach, mentor, and author. As president of Betof Associates, he does C-level executive and leadership team coaching. He also serves as executive coach for the Center for Creative Leadership and teaches for the Institute for Management Studies.

In 2007, Ed retired as worldwide vice president of talent management and CLO at Becton, Dickinson and Company. In addition, he served for eight years as the program director for the Conference Board's Talent and Organization Development Executive Council, and was a founding senior fellow and an academic director for the doctoral program designed to prepare chief learning officers at the University of Pennsylvania.

Ed is the author or co-author of five books, including *Leaders as Teachers: Unlock the Teaching Potential of Your Company's Best and Brightest, Leaders as Teachers Action Guide,* and *Just Promoted!: A Twelve-Month Roadmap for Success in Your New Leadership Role.* He is a frequent speaker on leadership and career topics and a former ATD Board member.

Nila Betof, PhD, is chief operating officer of the Leader's Edge/Leaders By Design. She has held several corporate C-suite and executive roles, including chief operating officer, chief human resources officer, and head of strategic planning. Her executive coaching work is primarily focused on senior leaders and emerging leaders.

Nila was the recipient of the 2011 Smart COO Award from *Smart CEO* magazine. She also served as president of the Forum of Executive Women, and currently serves on the Thirty-Percent Coalition and NextMove Dance boards.

Nila has authored numerous articles on leadership and is frequently sought as a speaker on leadership issues, especially on developing and retaining high-potential women leaders. She co-authored *Just Promoted!: A Twelve-Month Roadmap for Success in Your New Leadership Role.*